God's Gems

Jim Sinclair

This book exists because of the help and/or activities of several other people.

TERRY KING was the person who made the chance comment that started it all.

MIKE MURRAY made the computer program to add up sentences and factorise the numbers.

PASTOR DARRYL WILLIAMS, Senior pastor of the Melbourne Revival Fellowship has been a helpful source of information at many times.

PASTOR FRANK NANKIVILLE a pastor of the Revival Centres International, Melbourne was willing to give one to one instruction to an enthusiastic but raw beginner.

The young man from England who restarted the project when it was about to collapse is LEE FINNEY.

PASTOR CHRIS KERNAHAN of the Adelaide Revival Fellowship gave the project a push along at several critical times.

PASTOR MARK WATTCHOW, Senior pastor of the Christchurch, New Zealand, Revival Fellowship was a helpful and interested second set of eyes to correct my calculations.

LISA MASON designed the covers.

TOM NOBEL and IAN STEER did proof reading and editing of the text.

My Wife, NANCY, made the time available and kept the rest of the World from distracting me.

I offer my sincere thanks to all of you!

TABLE OF CONTENTS

Contents

Chapter 1: A Chance Comment...5

Chapter 2: Panin, Bullinger and Others 12

Chapter 3: Third John; First Gems...17

Chapter 4: A Mind Boggling Conclusion....................................30

Chapter 5: Twenty Years Later..39

Chapter 6: Elemental Truth...44

Chapter 7: The greatest surprise 52

Chapter 8: Counting on God's Fingers 59

Chapter 9: The Search For A Yardstick 66

Chapter 10: Gems of Proof 74

Chapter 11: The Patriarch's Numbers......................................80

Chapter 12: The Big Picture 146

Appendix 1 152

Appendix 2 156

Appendix 3 158

Appendix 4: Numerical gemstones discovered so far.........................161

OTHER BOOKS BY THE SAME AUTHOR 163

Chapter 1: A Chance Comment

This is a story of a search that began 42 years ago. Some gems have been found, and many more are yet to be discovered. It is a search that will not be completed for several more lifetimes, so others will need to take it up and continue the work. It is not a "climb every mountain and turn over every rock" type of search; it is more like "wade through mountains of numbers and find the gems of proof of non-random links". It all started with a chance comment – almost a 'throw-away line' – made to me that changed my life for ever.

In Australia, freedom of religion is enshrined in the Constitution. When that was written, the underlying thought was that because nobody has any proof of anything, everybody has a perfect right to believe whatever they want to believe. A side effect of that has been to make it socially unacceptable, or at least very bad manners, to ask anyone to prove what they believe in. When I was a child, people around me talked about a God, but nobody knew anything much about Him. The idea of an old man in the sky with a long white beard was common. Banjo Patterson's "What parson tellim you, ole Mister Dodd, tell you in Sunday-School? Big pfella God." was about as good as it got in those days. I can remember my mother talking about people who would go to Heaven and have "a thousand years of peace and safety!" but I can also remember being told, "Only perfect people go to Heaven, so forget about it, kid."

Right from the start, I was different: I wanted proof! As I was growing up I met religious people from time to time, and it was a pastime to argue with them. In most cases they had an unshakable faith, but no evidence. Their faith did not attract me at all: I wanted evidence! I knew that a world without a God could not possibly ever have an ultimate purpose, so although part of what they said sounded good to me, their lack of evidence repelled me. It can be very lonely and uncomfortable being different!

Science was a rising star in those days. All over the world there were scientists saying, "We are doing research that will make people live longer and longer". The pot of gold at the end of their rainbow was, "Give us enough money for research, and we will be able to make people live for ever!" In the 1950s they often had great successes, so their claim did have some point to it.

The scientists had the evidence; the scientific method is a disciplined way of collecting and proving evidence, but the end they offered was a mouldering body rotting to a heap of dust with no long-term purpose for anything. So, I liked the 'God' that religious people talked about, but was repelled by their lack of evidence; I liked the evidence that the scientific people talked about, but was repelled by the lack of purpose in anything they offered!

Not only was I different from the religious people, I was also different from the scientists. In the background of my young days there was always an unsatisfied hunger for purpose.

My father was a sheep farmer, and he wanted nothing else but to be a sheep farmer or grazier. His forebears were some of the first people to take a mob of sheep into the Port

Lincoln area. In the 1930s he farmed wheat in the Murray Mallee and was paying off a mortgage, but then the financial situation worsened and the bank foreclosed his mortgage. He never again borrowed money from a bank!

Then World War II broke out. My father enlisted in the RAAF and was given some basic training in radio technology. He worked on a bomber airfield out from Darwin, where his main tasks were to tune the transmitter and receiver of each aircraft every morning to the day frequency, and then in the evening to retune them to the night frequency. At the end of the war, Dad signed up for the Soldier Settlement Scheme, and five years later, when I was seven years old, we went to live on a block he could call his own. When I was ten years old my sister and I were playing in a back shed, and I unearthed some of Dad's wartime training manuals and exercise books. I was fascinated with one of them, and that book started what has become a lifetime interest for me.

After I left high school, everyone in the district expected me to complete my father's dream by working on the farm. While that may have been his dream, to me it was an enslavement that I went along with out of duty, not by choice. That must have shown, and when his health started to fail the farm was sold, and we moved to a small property where Dad could do as much or as little farming as he wanted. I was then free to get a job in the field of my interest. It wasn't really work; I was doing what I had previously done for a hobby, and was getting paid for it.

My father's vision of eternal life was a dynasty, a never-ending succession of descendants gradually building up a famous name in rural industry. I could never share that concept; to me, it was still not an ultimate purpose. A sheep farmer produces wool, which helps keep people warm; other farmers produce food, and that helps as well. There was a continual undercurrent of persuasion saying that farming was a respectable profession, inferring that farming or grazing was the only respectable profession. Meanwhile, there was a continual feeling gnawing away inside of me, saying that I was not doing anything of really permanent value.

So, I wanted a God, but was different from the religious people; I wanted evidence, but was different from the scientists; and now I was also different from my father's dream.

The work took me to Darwin, where I met Nancy. She turned out to be a kindred spirit, and we got married. Work then took us to Alice Springs, where we had good jobs and found people who were friendly to us. For the next few years we did all the typical things that young married couples do, but in a non-typical way. Both of us were continually looking for something worthwhile to give us an ultimate purpose to life, and everything we did was on a 'this will do for now' basis. We lived in Alice Springs for six and a half years, and our two sons were born there. Work then brought us to South Australia, at first as a temporary transfer, but then it became permanent. Three months after we moved here my father died, and we then looked after my mother and the small farming property on which they had lived. Because of my work, those tasks fell mainly on Nancy, who also carried on the full-time job of caring for our young children at home.

In all that time, neither of us found anything that would be a permanent purpose to our lives.

We didn't know it then, but in those days God was working on us behind the scenes. He had put us together in the first place, opening some opportunities and closing others. Only now, after years of experiencing the power of God in action, can we look back and understand what He did for us at that time.

There were religious people in Nancy's family on her father's side. She had a basic belief in a God, but didn't know where to find Him, and she knew that there was something special about the Bible, but didn't know exactly what it was. She had grown up with the scripture, "Jesus Christ the same yesterday, today and for ever" and had worked out for herself that the true church, if it existed, would agree with that scripture on three major points:-

- The people would follow the Bible.

- They would experience miracles of the same types that Jesus saw.

- There would be no crosses, candles or idolatry symbols.

I, on the other hand, had no particular respect for the Bible, but neither was I particularly against it. I could see that it had some stories about supernatural things, but I had grown up with the idea from my parents that 'supernatural' was spooky and was a good thing to keep away from.

One morning in March 1978, the car that Nancy was driving had an engine failure directly outside a vandalised public telephone box. She knocked on the doors of some local houses to ask if she could borrow a telephone, and at one house a lady named Jean said "Yes". While they waited for help (me) to arrive, Jean said to Nancy, "Do you believe in God?" "Yes, I do!" Nancy replied. Jean went on to say, "The Bible says, 'He who believes and is baptised shall be saved, but he who believes not shall be damned', and there are signs that follow believers. Where we fellowship…" and she named exactly the three points that Nancy had worked out would identify the true church. Nancy was shocked and excited all at once, and from then on could think of nothing else.

When she told me about it later that day, I was only mildly interested; it was her experience and an interesting story, but it wasn't the evidence that would mean something to me. We have since found out many times in many ways that where God is involved, a point that may be the key to life for one person may be of just passing interest to another who needs a different key.

A few days later, we arranged for Nancy to meet someone from the same Fellowship who had a bit more experience. I went along as well, not expecting anything more than just another religion. At one point in the conversation, Terry said to me, "There is a numeric code built into the text of the Bible that could not have been put there by any natural person!"

That statement was the key to life for me; suddenly I had evidence! From then on the whole world was different!

Suddenly the hunger for purpose was gone. I did not take it personally at first – "only perfect people go to Heaven", as I had been told many times – but the fact that somebody would go to Heaven and have eternal life was the ultimate purpose for life.

Chapter 2: Panin, Bullinger and Others

Come with me and you will see some gems but be warned; there are many imitations. There is a war going on, it is a funny sort of war, a spiritual war between the God who answers by fire and Satan the great imitator and the 'author of confusion'. The real gems are hard facts of testable and provable non-random links, the imitations are soft, sparkling, flashy presentations; exciting but they fail the test. The real gems are in the Bible's numeric code; the imitations are numerology and tricks with numbers. The Bible's numeric code when it is properly used is one of the sharpest weapons in the war against Satan and the weapon he would most like to blunt with imitations.

Before we start there is a decision you must make for yourself. Do you want to be on God's side or Satan's side? If you decide for God's side be sure that there is only one God who answers by fire; only one who can suspend the laws of physics and chemistry and actually do miracles. There are thousands of imitation gods who look enticing but actually do nothing. If you decide for God you must make a conscious effort to follow Him, the real one. If you have been honest and wholehearted the result will be that you will speak in tongues which is the experience described in chapter 2 of the Bible book of Acts as it happened to the original Apostles. When that has happened to you then you complete the contract by being baptised (completely immersed in water) which is a symbolic burial of your former life. If you never make a decision and just drift along you will drift into Satan's camp and never see the future that God seeks to offer you. If you follow any of the powerless gods of religion they will just as surely lead you into Satan's camp.

When Terry told me about the numeric code he actually knew very little more than the one fact that he told me. What gradually came to light over the following few weeks and months was that the existence of the code was widely accepted as an article of faith by the people in that fellowship but very few of them had any detailed knowledge of how it worked and almost none of them even thought about actually proving that the numbers they quoted were in any way anything other than chance events.

At that time the general understanding of the Bible's code was based on the writings of Ivan Panin. He was a mathematician who originally had been an agnostic who had set out to prove using mathematics that there was nothing supernatural about the Bible. After an extensive investigation he actually proved to himself that the converse was true, that there in fact had been a supernatural code built into the original Hebrew and Greek scriptures. After that he spent the rest of his life investigating that code and publishing his findings. He was born in Russia in 1855 and died in 1942 which, significantly, was four years before the first electronic computer went into service.

In the late 19th century there was considerable interest in Panin's discoveries and it lead to investigations by others, mainly in the eastern side of the United States of America, into subjects related to that. There was a book published under the title, "Number in Scripture" written by Ethelbert W. Bullinger which deals with the numeric value of the alphabetic characters of the Greek and Hebrew written languages and ties meaning to the numbers mainly by listing examples of how particular numbers associate with scriptures of particular types. Number in Scripture was first published in 1894 and had been reprinted several times since then. There is almost no overlap between the work of Ivan Panin and that of Bullinger but both are accepted as contributing to the general subject of, "Bible Numerics".

For me it was imperative, a matter of spiritual life or death, to identify exactly what was involved in the subject of Bible numerics and more specifically to prove that it was a genuinely non-random linking. At that time hard facts were rare and proof of anything almost did not exist. However, it was clear from almost the first moment when Terry had spoken to me that anyone who is motivated enough could collect the data and do the sums for themselves.

It must be made clear at this stage that there is a fairly constant stream of objections against the basic subject of Bible numerics claiming that it has never been proven. These objections are from people who don't want to believe in a supernatural God and who will cling to any excuse not to have to believe. The truth is that at the time the modern understanding of Bible numerics was being defined (late 19th century) the mathematical procedures that we now understand as 'modern probability theory' did not exist; the use of probability theory for quality control in factories and testing of results in scientific experiments only became feasible after the development of the electronic computer which had its first appearance in 1946. In the 19th century the rudimentary form of probability theory of that time only existed in gambling dens and race tracks.

The points that could be gleaned from talking to a number of different people were:-

- There is widely believed to be a hidden code of numbers built into the original text of the Hebrew Old Testament and the Greek New Testament.
- Both of those languages use the same written symbols for both letters of their alphabet and for numbers.
- The code is somehow related to addition of the total number values of a group of characters, perhaps each word or each sentence.
- All of the numbers from 1 to 13 and some of the higher prime numbers have a concept or meaning associated with them.
- For numbers 14 and above which have factors the meaning linked to them is related to the list of the factors.
- The numbers written in the Bible in plain language are also tied in with those same hidden meanings.
- The only 'proof' that anyone had of any of that was the probability figures that Ivan Panin had published in his books. Most of his sums had been done at close to the turn of the century and were not convincing when judged by the yard stick of modern probability theory.

That was the real starting point for my search.

Chapter 3: Third John; First Gems

The Third Epistle of John is the shortest book in the whole Bible; it is only 15 sentences. Whatever code is present has to be complete in each book so that is the book that needs the least work to prove whether a code exists or not.

Ye all who are reading this book will have come from a wide variety of backgrounds and have a wide range of capabilities and degree of interest in mathematics. The story becomes fairly heavily mathematical for the next few pages; if you don't want to get that closely involved you will be able to skim through to a summary at (Kindle 15%). If on the other hand it is important for you to check my sums Appendix 1 at the end of the main story gives samples of the Greek texts that I used as source documents. There should be enough data in that Appendix for you to reconstruct my calculation. Note a practicality that for individual readers these percentage figures may be up to one or two different in some devices; as a general rule however if you find that the 15% figure suggested above turns out to be a bit different you could expect that all the Kindle percentages mentioned would tend to be biased about the same amount in the same direction.

For the first few weeks my attempts to find anything at all non-random were very much stumbling around in the dark. In a lot of his work Ivan Panin had focussed on the number 7 and shown that particular scriptures had a lot more features of the number 7 than should have been possible by blind chance. In the wider world every number from 1 to 13 has a linkage to some meaning so it is not possible to focus on any one in particular. Gradually over those weeks my attention was focussed on the repetition of factors as a feature to look for. Even that did not bring good results at first.

The source of data was a problem. It was a known starting point that the code was in the original languages which in this case was an ancient version of Greek. Strong's Concordance has a Greek dictionary in the back of it and there were some words in that but not all. The next easiest source was an, "Interlinear Bible" by George Ricker Berry in which the Greek words are written with the nearest equivalent English word immediately under it.

The Kindle program does not support the publication of Greek text in a basically English language book so it is not possible to show the sentence in its original form; if it is sufficiently important to you it would be possible to acquire a set of Greek characters and reconstruct the sentence from the following. In the Interlinear Bible the Greek words of the first sentence of Third John are:-

The first word is the single letter 'omicron' which is translated as, 'The'. The second word is, 'pi, rho, epsilon, sigma, beta, upsilon, tau, epsilon, rho, omicron, stigma' which is translated as, 'elder'. The third word is, 'gamma, alpha, iota, psi' which is translated as the man's name, 'Gaius'. The fourth word is, 'tau, psi' which is translated as, 'the'. The fifth word is, 'alpha, gamma, alpha, pi, eta, tau, psi' which is translated as, 'beloved'. The sixth word is, 'omicron, nu' which is translated as, 'whom'. The seventh word is, 'epsilon, gamma, omega' which is translated as, 'I'. The eighth word is, 'alpha, gamma, alpha, pi, omega' which is translated as, 'love'. The ninth word is, 'epsilon, nu' which is translated as, 'in' and the tenth word is, 'alpha, lambda, eta, theta, epsilon, iota, alpha' which is translated as, 'truth'.

The numbers that correspond to these letters are:-

70/ 80,100,5,200,2,400,300,5,100,70,6/ 3,1,10,700/ 300,700/ 1,3,1,80,8,300,700/ 70,50/ 5,3,800/ 1,3,1,80,800/ 5,50/ 1,30,8,9,5,10,1

Adding up each of the words individually gives:-

70__1268__714__1000__1093__120__808__885__55 __64

The total of all these is 6077. The factors are 59 x 103 which does not seem like a numerically significant result.

There were lots of loose ends in all that. One of the simplest was that somebody had suggested that the whole Bible should be written in uppercase letters. That makes only one difference to that first sentence, the final letter of the second word. For the 'S' sound the Greek language uses the letter 'sigma' except when it is the last letter of a word when (stigma) is used which is a character that looks like the English 's" with a long tail; however, stigma is only a lowercase letter. When it is all uppercase 'Sigma' is used for both sigma and stigma. The numeric value of stigma is 6, the numeric value of 'Sigma' is 200. If that sentence was all uppercase its total value would be 6271 which is a prime number.

There are known to be spelling errors in these sentences. The oldest manuscripts we have to refer to are thought to be third or fourth generation copies and by now nobody knows which is the original spelling. Strong's Concordance shows the following alternatives for this sentence.

- For the fifth word (alpha, gamma, alpha, pi, eta, tau, omicron, stigma) whose numbers total 469 instead of 1093.
- For the eighth word (alpha, gamma, alpha, pi, alpha, omega) whose numbers are 886 instead of 885.

These two extra alternatives meant that the total number of possible answers goes up to 8 (each extra alternative doubles the number of possibilities). The extra possibilities are listed in the following table which can be read with your reader turned to the right hand landscape direction. None of these have very much numeric significance by themselves. There were however more spelling alternatives to be tried.

The extra variations of spelling lead to these numbers:-

70	1268	714	1000	469	120	808	885	55	64	= 5453	= 7 x 19 x 41
70	1268	714	1000	1093	120	808	886	55	64	= 6078	= 2 x 3 x 1013
70	1268	714	1000	469	120	808	886	55	64	= 5454	= 2 x 27 x 101
70	1462	714	1000	663	120	808	885	55	64	= 5841	= 9 x 11 x 59
70	1462	714	1000	663	120	808	886	55	64	= 5842	= 2 x 23 x 127

The alternative in which the second word is 1462 and the fifth is 469 is not a valid possibility.

The British and Foreign Bible Society have published a New Testament in the ancient Greek text that the original Bible was written in. The title of their book is, (Eta, Kappa, Alpha, Iota, Nu, Eta, Delta, Iota, Alpha, Theta, Eta, Kappa,

Eta) which has one very significant variation from the Interlinear Bible; The second word of this sentence is written all in uppercase letters!

Counting all the possible alternatives there were a total of 72 ways in which they could be combined but some combinations were not valid and some caused the same total to appear in two different sums. When all combinations of all the possible alternatives were tried there were a total of 28 different sums and the gem is as shown in the following illustration which also is displayed in the right hand landscape form.

The numerically correct spelling in the Greek language for the first sentence of the Third Epistle of John is

Ο ΠΡΕΣΒΥΤΕΡΟΣ Γαιω τω αγαπητω ον εγω αγαπαω εν αληθεια

The numbers for each of those words are:-

70   1462   714   1000   1093   120   808   886   55   64

The sum of all these numbers is 6272 and the factors are $2^7 \times 7^2$. From the point of view of repeating of factors, it is the best possible combination; the factors themselves are significant to the extent of $2^6 \times 7$ but also the index of each one is the same as the numeral of the other one. From the repeated factors angle that number has one chance in 6,272 but because it is a one out of 28 pick the actual significance has to be reduced. 6272 / 28 = 224. Even taking account of all the spelling errors that have gathered over the years one chance in 224 is still definitely significant. (This is not the true way to work out that probability calculation but it was the simplistic way I looked at it then. The real proof came later with the control group.)

For me privately the moment those factors appeared was the spiritual life or death moment. It was not something that anyone could tell the world about but from that moment on the truth of all they had said about Bible numerics was fixed. This was hard evidence!

There was still some work to be done; the theory said that if that was a special number there had to be only one of them. It was still required to work through all 27 other numbers and prove that none of them had factors like that one; and that was how it worked out. All the others were either prime numbers or the list of factors ended in a large prime number. 6272 was the gem and the only one for that sentence.

Mike Murray is a friend who lived in Whyalla at the time. He was, and still is, an expert on the uses of personal computers. When he saw the working out and the result of that first sentence he was able to draft a program using the BASIC language (all the rage 42 years ago) to do the same calculation and print the results. To do it he needed the whole of Third John to be translated into numbers with all the alternative spellings; that kept me busy for some weeks.

Mike's program worked and printed out results. Sentence number 2 had no correct results but number 3 had a result almost as convincing as number 1. When the program got to number 5 it started printing but Mike had to stop it when the wad of paper was a couple of centimetres thick. It was a long sentence and we worked out afterwards that the full list of answers would have been about 15,000 sums and in that range there would have been several numbers that would have looked numerically significant. That was a very valuable lesson to have learned at that time.

For sentence number 3 the gem was 2^3 x 3^5 x 5; the total is 9720. The probability is 2^2 x 3^4 x 3 x 5 which equals one in 4860. There were 96 sums but some of them duplicated the answers so there were 80 alternatives and the final probability was about one in 60.

The spelling of that numerical gem is shown in the following illustration which also is in landscape format.

The numerically correct spelling in the Greek language for the third sentence of the Third Epistle of John is

εχασην λιαν ερχομενων αδελφων και αρτυρεω σου τη αληθεια καθωσ σου εν αληθεια περιπατεω.

The numbers for these words are:-

| 764 | 91 | 1720 | 1390 | 31 | 1746 | 670 | |
| 308 | 64 | 836 | 600 | 55 | 64 | 1381 | total 9720 |

Soon after that time my work was changed to include radio field strength measurement and a programmable calculator was added to my toolkit. It was only rarely needed for work purposes and could be programmed to calculate the factors of big numbers. To work through all of the other ten sentences took almost three years of spare time.

Only about half of the other sentences gave any significant result. Some of them were like sentence number 5; too long and with too many alternatives to show a clear answer. Others clearly did not show any answer at all. Of the ones that did give a repeating set of factors after the raw probability figure had been divided by the number of sums the final figure was close to a chance of one in 10 which is usually taken as 'doubtful'.

One of the sentences looked impressive at first but turned out to be a false hope. It was sentence number seven, which talks about the resistance due to Diotrophes. At first I made a calculation of 8192 for the sentence total which is 2^{13} but later when I was searching for the combination of spellings I could not find the combination that produced that result; the nearest I could find was one that was 100 less. That was both a great disappointment and a valuable lesson for me; the gematria aspect of the code is an error detection code with similar characteristics to parity coding used internally in computers but the original text does not contain enough information to be an error correction code. (A comparable example is 'forward error correction' which uses enough extra bits to provide parity information in a grid format.)

The results of my attempts to tell other people about my findings were patchy at best. Most people could not follow the steps that lead to these answers and of those that could follow they would usually say something like, "One in ten is not really significant is it?" A control group of some sort was needed.

All of the results that had worked out had included one or more low prime numbers in their list of factors; the first four are 2, 3, 5 and 7. These four prime numbers multiplied together give 210. One way to set up a control group is to take every answer of every sum that had been worked out before and add 211 to each then test for factors of them. The theory was that to do that would destroy the genuine pattern that had been shown in the first set of answers. If that pattern was actually a chance event, then it would be replaced by another equally significant looking pattern. If it was not replaced by another pattern that would be evidence that the original was supernaturally inspired.

The result of that was as hoped for; it destroyed the original pattern and did not replace it with another one. For each sentence of the control group the most significant looking set of factors had a high value prime number at the end of the row and the probability was never more than about one in 2.5. For me that was proof of the supernatural origin of the code.

Despite the extra certainty of the control group test the most common comments either showed a lack of understanding of what was being tested or brought a comment something like, "Why do you need to prove it; I thought Panin did that long ago?" or, "We know it works; why bother?"

The people who were dismissive of this numerical proof of the supernatural were not dis-interested in salvation and eternal life. There are many people who seek the God with evidence but there are a wide range of things which are seen as convincing evidence to different people; for each of us there is a particular key item or action that proves God to each one and that thing, whatever it is, is different for different people. We in our family had that experience between the two of us in the very early days of our contact with the Biblical God. There are only a few people who are affected by Bible numerics the way it happened to me. It is still lonely being different but not as before; the gnawing hunger for purpose is gone, God gives purpose. I am aware that there must be other people in the World who need this numeric coding as their key to God; I am looking for them but haven't found him or her yet.

The summary of this chapter is:-

- There are two sentences that can be shown to have a definitely non-random pattern in their spelling.
- There are several other sentences that probably have a coding related to those two.
- When the sentences of Third John are tested against a control group there is a very clear and definite difference between the original and the control groups.
- It would be possible for a linguist or similar person to use this procedure to identify the original spelling of some of the sentences (mostly the shorter ones) in the Bible.

Chapter 4: A Mind Boggling Conclusion

I only talked to a few people about that study and none of them were anyone outside the Fellowship. Part of the reason for that was that most people seemed to be not particularly interested; the other part was that I was very aware that the whole subject could be very easily polluted; the proof depends on rigorous testing of all possible combinations and you know for a start that all except one of the sums for each sentence will produce a fruitless answer. On the other hand, an enthusiastic number cruncher could produce results which would look impressive but the real proof would be lacking.

Personally I had the surety of my results and that was useful for my faith but in daily life I put the numeric sums to one side and got on with activities that were more main stream in the Fellowship. I was working in a radio technical job which forces you into contact with a whole range of scientific subjects and I found myself almost living in two worlds. In the Fellowship I found that people had evidence and that was all they wanted but for work I was in the scientific and academic world; that seems to attract people who don't want to believe in a God and who will weave atheism into their activities at every chance they get. I didn't really fit very well into either world so I kept a low profile and used the time to learn all I could about the God of evidence.

By that time, I and all our family had been baptised and had received the Holy Spirit; We had spoken in languages we had not learned and were using those languages regularly to allow our spirits to contact the spirit of God. That process was evidence on a daily basis so the evidence of the numerics testing had a bit less of a life-and-death urgency about it.

In those days (early 1980s) the common wisdom among Fellowship people was that the Bible's numeric code applied to the Bible and nothing else. The idea was persuasive; it was a means of proving the supernatural inspiration of the Bible and there was no reason to look for supernatural inspiration in anything else. For work however I kept finding by accident facts that matched the numeric code to some parts of the natural world. That happened most often when solid state electronics came into contact with some odd side effects of chemistry.

The first and most obvious of them was the principle of eight. If you look at the chemical periodic table and think about each element in turn the change that happens when you move from one element to the next is that there is a proton added to the nucleus of the atom each time and an extra electron in the outer orbital. Each time the atom has built up to have 8 electrons in its outermost orbital, when the next proton and electron are added, the atom starts a new orbital outside the previous one. By a tremendous coincidence the Bible numeric link to the number 8 means among other things, "A new start!"

In modern times a lot of the questions about geography have been answered by the new subject of, "Plate tectonics" which was started by someone in South America finding a fossilised tooth in Patagonia which they could identify as related to the teeth of wombats in Australia. That indicated that Australia was once joined to South America. There were a few other small clues like that one and obviously the modern understanding of plate tectonics includes a lot more than just a few small clues. For me the 'coincidence' surrounding the number 8 was equivalent to the Patagonian tooth.

The next match to show up was related to the element carbon. In the natural world carbon is the key element for life, we are described as, "A carbon based life form" so it is reasonable to think of carbon as a symbol for the living part of the natural creation. Carbon has valency of 4 and has 4 electrons in its outermost orbital. In the Bible's numeric code, the number 4 is linked to, "The natural creation!"

For some time, I discounted these and some other things as interesting coincidences. I respected the opinion of the people who quoted the common answer; but the coincidences kept appearing!

Time rolled on. It was actually about 20 years before I did any purposeful testing of that list of coincidences and then it was at the end of a rather weird train of events.

I left employment in the broadcasting transmitter field in 1986 and started working up a business in radio communications. One of the sidelines that was fairly successful at certain times of the year was the hiring of HF land mobile transceivers to off-the-beaten-track tourists in four-wheel drive vehicles. Mostly the hire period would be for a month at a time, the people would bring their vehicle, I would set the transceiver in a place convenient to them, clamp an aerial onto the bull-bar and connect it all up. I would then encourage them to make an initial test call to the relevant

Flying Doctor base and when that was done they would wave goodbye and I would next see them a month later.

The HF band (short wave radio for most people) has always had a sort of lunatic fringe quality about it. Under ideal conditions it is capable of carrying signals further around the surface of the Earth than is possible with any of the other bands but success very much depends on choosing the correct band of those available and operating at the best time of the day or night. Band conditions can change from day to day and larger variations are possible over periods of several days. Success very much depends on having operated on the channel fairly regularly within the previous few days and familiarity with the recent day to day conditions is critical to successful use in an emergency. When the travellers came to return the equipment they would all too often say, "We didn't ever have to use it, but it was good to have it just in case!"

That statement worried me, I was giving them a false sense of security which if they had ever had a real emergency could actually have been a hazard to them. At first I tried talking to individual travellers asking them to do check calls every few days at least and daily if possible but that statement kept cropping up.

I next tried to draw a diagram which turned out to be a map of Australia with information about emergency communications that will work from each location. When it was eventually ready for printing the printer had to make a batch of 5,000 to justify setting up his equipment. I really only had a need for a few dozens so I tried to find other businesses operating in the HF land mobile field who may be able to sell the others. For most of them it was a dead issue except for one shop in the eastern suburbs of Melbourne who was able to sell 7,000 altogether in one tourist season. It is only of historical interest now, it included predictions of conditions in the 1992 winter season which was expected to be the sunspot minimum of that cycle. The map was technically correct but very intricate and too complicated to be much use for non-technical people to use without instruction.

My next try was to write something that would be useful to a non-technical person if they were caught in the situation of having an emergency without the daily use that makes the HF band effective. I worked from the point of view of treating the transceiver as a mystery box and concentrating the story on what happens to the signal after it leaves the transmitting aerial until it gets to the receiver aerial. The story kept getting more and more complicated; after it had got to 120 pages and was not yet finished I mentally stood back and took stock. My original aim had been to write perhaps 10 to 20 pages of explanation specific to the use of the HF band then take it to a printer who could make a small number of copies and bind each of them into a reasonably robust cover. The problem started when I thought about people wanting to keep the booklet as a memento of their trip; they really should have a bit of explanation of the basics of what a radio signal actually is and so the complication started.

The other option was to widen the focus a bit, include reference to bands other than the HF band, try to interest other radio communication users and see if there was a commercial publisher who would sell it to a wider market. It was taken up by the Australian office of McGraw-Hill, they wanted even more general interest content and the result was sold as, "How Radio Signals Work". The final book was a long way different from the original need which was to explain emergency communications to unfamiliar users on the HF band. A couple of years later it was reprinted in USA and has apparently been sold in many English speaking countries around the World.

I still had the problem of people who would hire a transceiver and then not use it, I began to wonder if another book more specifically focussed on propagation of signals would fill the need. I drafted another manuscript, sent it off to the Australian office of McGraw-Hill and heard absolutely nothing for 8 months.

Our daughter, Ruth, had gone to Canada and had met a young man named Tony. In due course we received an email from Ruth which told us that she and Tony had decided to get married and outlined the steps they had taken so far. We did not have the money for a trip to Canada so I sent back a reply that said we were delighted to hear it but they would have to make all the arrangements themselves. I ended the message with the statement, "It would take a miracle for us to get there!"

After I sent off that email the next one I opened was from the New York office of McGraw-Hill; an offer of a publishing contract and the first line of the offer was an advanced payment of $US 3,000. At that time the Australian Dollar was worth about 55 US cents. The price was almost exactly the cost of two round-the-world air tickets.

The background was quite obvious but with mind boggling implications; it was a message from God;

Get passports,

Buy tickets,

Get on the plane

Go to the other side of the World

Don't ask questions,

You will be told what to do when you get there.

I broke the news to Nancy by saying, "We have just been sent to Canada!"

Later I was in conversation with a fellowship member and when I told him about that he asked, "Was it awfully hard to take that risk?" My answer at that time was, and still is, "It is easy if you can be sure it is God that is directing the operation". In this case the train of events was so weird and unlikely that it had to be God doing it so it was all very easy for us.

Some time later, Ruth and Tony came to Australia and Tony has since been baptised and received the Holy Spirit. We found out later that an essential part of that move was that Tony, who had grown up in a rural part of northern Ontario, had met us and got to know us at the time of the wedding.

With the benefit of hindsight, we can see that the whole action right back to the four-wheel drive tourists who did not use their transceivers was a carefully planned sequence of events that would end up with Tony and Ruth being in Australia and both involved in the Kingdom of God. In the normal course of events I would never have even considered setting out to write a book in the hope that someone might publish it; I failed English in the final year of High School.

Much later when the list of 'coincidences' became too long to ignore I started trying to think of ways to tell the story; but what was the story? At the Universal scale, if the chemical elements really were tied in with the Bible's numeric code then it was implied that God must have had the text of the Bible available in the most minute detail before He created the Universe! That suggestion is mind boggling but there are some scriptures that point to that possibility. God introduced Himself to Moses as, "I AM, I see the end from the beginning." The gospel of John starts with, "In the beginning was the word, and the word was with God and the word was God" and a few verses later, "The word was made flesh and dwelt among us" and it was the Word of God that created the physical Universe.

At the sub-microscopic scale, we are aware that sub-atomic particles don't actually touch each other. They are attracted and kept in place by force fields. We can measure the strength and direction of these force fields but there is nobody anywhere in the human race who has the faintest idea of what those force fields actually are. Three thousand years ago when the ancient Greeks first found the electric force they named it that way. The 'el' part of the word means 'God' so a literal translation of the word, 'electric' would be, "God's force". After 3,000 years of experiments by many different people working in many different languages in many countries, no-one has ever had a better suggestion. The idea that God could be directing and supervising the movement of individual sub-atomic particles all over the whole Universe is also mind boggling and there are probably very few people who could easily come to terms with it.

Chapter 5: Twenty Years Later

The chemical periodic table has changed and developed over the years. When I was in High School in the late 1950s it was introduced to us late in the final year. At that time, it only had eight columns and a couple of lists of elements that were awkward and did not fit in any of the eight columns. We learned that it somehow explained valency, which was something that we had spent most of that year working on. In those days probably even the experts were a bit hazy on the positions of electrons in the orbitals.

At about the start of the 21st century there was a general feeling that the table should actually have 18 columns; the extra 10 being columns of the transition elements. That eventually became the official layout. Since that time there have been some times when the periodic table is presented with 32 columns and in that case the extra columns are to accommodate the rare earth (lanthanide) elements and the newly manufactured trans-uranium elements. These changes make the table better able to illustrate reality but they have had an unfortunate side effect. In the original eight column presentation the column numbers were directly related to the number of electrons in the outermost (chemical valency) orbitals. The changes to larger numbers of columns have masked the relevance to the number of electrons in the outermost orbital.

It was late 2008 before I looked seriously at the possibility of a non-random linkage between chemical elements and Bible numerics. My first thought was that the match would be to the column groups and I tried to define the common properties of each group. At that time, I did not know whether I should be looking for a match with valency numbers, with oxidation states or with numbers of electrons; the three parameters are closely related so I was carrying on three investigations in parallel for some time. There were a few examples where the match was obvious and easy to define. Matching element number 1 (hydrogen) to the presence of God was easy, it is almost everywhere in the Universe, it is a powerful reagent in both the chemical and the nuclear senses and is almost never visible in the elemental form. The inert gases could also be matched to 'a new start' and carbon fitted well with 'the natural creation'.

I can remember being quite excited when I looked closely at the properties of nitrogen and found all the ways it matched with the 'grace of God' and following that on with the finding that shell fish form an outer layer around their bodies of a dead chemical, calcium carbonate, whereas the bones of the higher animals are living organisms whose strength depends on a calcium and phosphorus based chemical. I must admit to a quite un-scientific emotional involvement in the search; I wanted to find a pattern; whereas a truly scientific researcher is supposed to not care about whether the result is positive or negative so long as it can be shown to be provably non-random by established statistical methods. I was aware right from the start that the total number of properties of all the elements is a prodigious number and it would be possible to form a very impressive looking pattern simply by cherry picking the data.

It was not all that hard to match fluorine and some of the other halogens (seven electrons) to the cleaning and disinfecting power of the Holy Spirit and there are about four ways in which magnesium and calcium (two electrons) can be matched to 'separation' which is the Bible numeric match to the number 2. Sodium (one electron) which is an active reagent and spread all over the World in sea water and common salt is almost as well matched to the presence of God as hydrogen is. The next element below carbon in column 14 is silicon and it is widespread in the Earth's crust as silicon dioxide; in the same sense that carbon is matched to the living part of the natural creation silicon, which is also a number 4 element, is equally matched to the non-living part. The elements with 6 electrons are in the column with oxygen and sulphur, the match with natural mankind is less obvious that some of the others but in the sense that mankind without God is intent on short term goals, will destroy other things to make them work and the effect of oxygen is to release energy by burning up the fuel; it is possible to match them up with that key.

The number 3 tricked me for some time. The English language words that it is matched to are 'completeness' or 'fullness' and neither of those words seemed to be particularly related to the elements in that column. Eventually I went to the Strong's Concordance and looked for what the original Christians had understood from the meanings in the original Greek.

'Complete' is translated from word number 4137 (pi, lambda, eta, rho, omicron, omega) which is defined as, "to make replete, i.e. (lit.) to cram (a net), level up (a hollow), or (fig.) to furnish (or imbue, diffuse, influence), satisfy, execute (an office), finish (a period or task), verify (or coincide with a prediction), etc.: accomplish x after, (be) complete, end, expire, fill (up), fulfil, (be, make) full (come), fully preach, perfect, supply.

The closely related word number 4138 (pi, lambda, eta, rho, omega, mu, alpha) is defined as; repletion or completion, i.e. (subj.) what fills (as contents, supplement, copiousness, multitude), or (obj.) what is filled (as container, performance, period):- which is put in to fill up, piece that filled up, fulfilling, full, fullness.

When I first read through all that, it was fairly confusing at first but, suddenly one part of it made beautiful sense. The original eight column periodic table was shown as columns 1 and 2 on the left hand side then a gap then columns 3 to 8 towards the right with a separate list of transition elements placed below the gap. What the Greeks had understood was 'a multitude' that would 'fill up a hollow'; the multitude was the transition elements and the 'hollow' was the gap in between column 2 and column 3.

It was very obvious that the fit between the Bible's code numbers and the elements at the top of the eight column table could be made spectacularly good but the matching ran out quickly for the heavier elements in each column. In addition, most of the transition elements did not have valency of three, as would be required for a real fit with the Bible's code. (I found much later that it is common for the rare earth elements at the heavier end of their range to have three as their valency but I didn't know it at that time.) The match was by no means complete but I thought it was enough to be noticed.

At that time, I had no intention of writing another book about anything. My intention was to use that information to talk to and hopefully convince some of the technical and scientific people I met from time to time. I soon found out that most of those sort of people are wilfully ignorant of God and in fact of anything supernatural; those who shared the feeling I had felt are extremely rare indeed. The most common replies I got were; from those who had previously heard about the numeric code, "It is unproven and no more significant than any other numerology;" or from others, "The Bible is myths and legends written by ignorant desert dwellers thousands of years ago." The small proportion who were willing to think at all about what I had found generally dismissed it as a few coincidences in the presence of a much larger number of elements that did not fit. That all makes me a weirdo of a very rare breed; I can live with that, but I cling to the notion that I am not the only one. I haven't found the others yet but he/she must be somewhere; God would not have bothered building this intricate and complex tapestry into the natural creation without it being needed as the key to eternal life for somebody!

I was mentally putting the whole subject away; it had been an interesting exercise for me but that was about all. In a casual conversation I talked about it to a young man in the Fellowship whom I had met a few times some years before. He had since gone to live in England; suddenly he looked intently at me and said, "That's Huge!"

Chapter 6: Elemental Truth

I was privately convinced of the reality of the tie between numerics and chemicals even 'though I was not able to explain it convincingly to anyone except that young man from England. To prove it I needed more evidence.

The strategy was to make a match with each one of the over 90 elements individually. That would be quite involved and take a long time; but it would not be impossible, just tedious. The first requirement was a reliable listing of all the properties of all the elements. Several of the more famous Universities publish lists of that type on the internet; it was at first difficult to know which ones are the reputable ones. It turned out that a few were obviously copies of others; the problem of that was to know which was the original and which were the copies. The selection method was to look at all the website entries for a particular element, and only use those properties that showed up in more than one of the websites. A printed encyclopaedia that we had owned for many years was also an excellent second opinion for all the information from the internet.

There was a listing from an Israeli Government Department of Science and Technology that was different from all the others; it did not list properties; it was concentrated on detailing the energy state within the orbital makeup of each atom. Of the others, one of the most comprehensive was a listing from the Los Alamos National Laboratory in the United States of America; that became the reference and properties from it were used if they could be confirmed by any of the other sites.

With attention to the individual elements starting at number 1 the properties of hydrogen and how they matched to the presence of God had already been worked out; that was simple. The investigation for helium took a lot more time; it is an inert gas but it does not have an eight electron outer shell as for all the other inert gases; its electron make-up is two electrons in one orbital and because that is a closed shell its valency is zero. The research dipped into the history of the concept of zero and the numbering systems used by the ancient Hebrews and Greeks and also into astronomy for a physical analogue for the Biblical concept of a lake of eternal fire. If each of the other 90 elements was going to take that long this was going to be a long project!

Fortunately, the definition and matching of the next 8 was a lot more straight-forward than had been the case for helium. For all except boron the matching was obvious. The next series started well for sodium and magnesium but then struck trouble.

Aluminium should have been related to the number 3 but there was no way it would fit; it would have fitted easily with number 2, its corrosion resistance comes from a layer of oxide on its surface; or it could have fitted with the number 4 for two reasons, it is chemically a major component of clay minerals and therefore a signature element for the natural creation in the same way as silicon is, or as the pure metal it is a major part of modern technology. For number 3 however it just would not match.

I spent a lot of time wrestling with aluminium but the more I studied it the more I found that it was an element with clear negative matching. It was strongly matched to a number of the Bible code but the number it was matched to was not the number of its outer shell electrons. Eventually I was forced to accept the negative matching and put aluminium aside and the project raced ahead for the next 7 elements up to calcium. All except argon and potassium were fairly obviously matched to their own Bible code number and those two were still positively matched but not so strongly as the earlier ones had been. It was then time to investigate the transition elements. It was also the time when the project was developing into a book length document; the explanation for the matching of each element was a half a page to a page of text so there was going to be 70 to 80 pages if there was no more than just a list of the elements.

Planning for a book was quite different from just making a list of elements that match the Bible code. A book needs to be self-explanatory, so there would need to be some extra sections added to the list. A most essential addition would be a brief account of how atoms are constructed, what is a proton, what is an electron and what is a neutron.

With regard to the transition elements there was quite a delay in working out what each element was actually doing and what the arrangement of electrons is. For that purpose, the Israeli government website was invaluable, it decoded the electron positions and energy levels into orbitals and told which were capable of being involved in chemical reactions.

The first series of transition elements (which are all metals) starts with another progression of valency numbers (and available electrons) which runs from scandium with three electrons to manganese with seven electrons. All of those elements can be related to the Bible numeric concepts for those numbers; for scandium and titanium the match is less obvious but for the latter three it is first class.

After the number seven of that progression the wheels fell off the cart. The next element is iron, then cobalt, nickel, copper and zinc. If that series had continued there would have been 8 electrons for iron ranging up to 12 for zinc but in fact the electron numbers turn around and go back down again with 6 for iron ranging down to 2 for zinc. That reversal matched the elements with Bible numerics, iron can be strongly matched to the works of mankind, there are properties of nickel that astronomers know about that show nickel should be matched to the natural creation and zinc with its world-wide use for galvanizing is very clearly matched to separation.

It took some days to find the reason why that reversal should occur; apparently electrons which are alone in an orbital by themselves can be involved in chemical reactions but those which are in a paired orbital will not. That is something which should apply to all atoms but only has a noticeable effect on these few transition metals and a few of the lanthanides. The elements in the series from scandium to manganese are building up orbitals with unpaired electrons but from then on extra electrons form pairs so that the number of unpaired electrons is reduced.

Tricky?

Yes, but there were lots more tricks to come.

The element copper was the next trick. It would not match to anything of numeric significance but it had properties that were clearly important in the Bible; it is associated with compromise and pollution of God's principles. Numerically it was the first of a new class of elements, it had to be described as 'indeterminate'.

For the rest of the elements in that series they could all be related to the relevant Bible code number but none of the associations were glaringly obvious. In the next series the column 1 element is rubidium which can be strongly matched to number one. Next after that is strontium which apart from its chemical similarity to calcium is actually another example of the 'indeterminate' class as for copper.

The second series of transition elements displays an even more intricate trickiness than the pairing of electrons. There is an anomaly with a double anomaly in the middle of the row which focusses attention on technetium and which enables that element to illustrate the crucifixion and resurrection of Jesus Christ!

The rest of the elements in that series from ruthenium to xenon are a mixed bunch. Three of them, ruthenium, cadmium and iodine strongly match the number of available electrons to the Bible code number. There are another six which can be matched but in which the clarity of the match is lower and another two, rhodium and antimony which share the 'indeterminate' class with copper and strontium. Palladium in the lower matched group has an interesting property; in a sense it can be said to have an outer orbital with zero electrons, the next inner orbital has the stable number of 18 electrons and when heated the element will allow hydrogen to diffuse through it. A story could be told (but not proven) of the $2 \times 9 = 18$ illustrating "separation" and "finality", the zero indicating the lake of eternal fire and the one for hydrogen indicating the presence of God.

One of my granddaughters when she was four years old asked, "Could God go to hell and come back again?" I had to think about that for a while; my reply was, "He probably could if He wanted to but He probably would not want to". The diffusion of hydrogen through heated palladium may be an indication of the answer to her question.

There is yet one more, tricky story, this one is in the lanthanide group of elements in the next series. The first element after lanthanum itself is cerium which has a unique property, it will adjust its electron arrangement when extreme pressure is applied. In its fourth orbital when pressure is low it has 19 electrons but under very high pressure that number changes to 20. Further along the series europium has 25 electrons in its fourth orbital and the next element, gadolinium also has 25 in its fourth orbital, the extra electron for gadolinium sits in the fifth orbital making it have 9 instead of 8 electrons. The next element in the series is terbium which has 27 electrons in its fourth orbital and 8 in its fifth.

In the trans-uranium elements, the series has the fifth orbital building from 18 to 32 electrons in a similar fashion to the fourth orbital in the lanthanides. The electron sharing between the fifth and sixth orbitals of the trans-uranium elements is less rigidly fixed than is the case for the lanthanides but we find that there are no orbitals with exactly 19 electrons and there are no orbitals with exactly 26 electrons. The combined result is that there is nowhere in the presently known Universe where an orbital has exactly 26 electrons. If the unique pressure response of cerium had not existed there would also have been no orbitals with exactly 19 electrons.

What is actually observed is that 26 is the only number missing from the list. 26 = 2 x 13; those factors are symbolic of "sanctification" for number 2 and "rebellion" for number 13. God does not allow them to exist together in the same orbital.

There are two elements among the lanthanides which can be classed with aluminium. Cerium and holmium are both strongly matched to a number which is different from that indicated by the electron configuration. The others of the group heavier than gadolinium are all weakly matched to the number 3.

After the lanthanides there is another group of transition elements which have very mixed matching to the Bible code. Four are strongly matched, two are weakly matched, two are indeterminate and one is clearly negative.

After them come the heavy metals, thallium, lead and bismuth. All the elements heavier than bismuth are radioactive and only exist in the modern world as decay products of the radioactivity of the primeval stock of either uranium or thorium. Two of them have such short half-lives that a pure sample of them has never been observed although their presence can be demonstrated by the radiation they produce. Of the 14 elements between thallium and plutonium five can be strongly matched to the Bible code, five can be weakly matched and four are indeterminate.

When the list was finished of the 94 elements checked, 40 of them could be strongly matched to the Bible numeric number of their available electrons. That number included two that were the result of the pairing of electrons so there were 38 that are beyond all reasonable doubt. There are another 35 (37 if the pairing of electrons is not allowed for) which are associated with the numeric code but less strongly matched; 15 are indeterminate and 4 are clearly negatively matched.

Chapter 7: The greatest surprise

It took about 18 months to convert the list of elements into a book manuscript. The list was really only half the story; there needed to be a first chapter explaining the parts of an atom that were being written about; there was also to be a chapter about the original investigation of the periodic table columns and there needed to be something about the way probabilities would be calculated. As I worked through the first group of transition elements I kept bumping into facts about those elements being alloyed with iron to make steel and those facts eventually became a chapter on their own. There was also going to be a chapter on the numeric matching of some of the simpler compounds of those elements. Another chapter would be about the mentions of elements in the Bible and the symbolic scriptural facts which are not always the same as the numeric matches.

My original intent was that this should be a reference book, filled with facts and very little padding. The facts would be presented in a way that they could be easily accessible for checking. The original manuscript had an index as every good reference book should have.

As I was working through the manuscript I became aware that there were a lot of scientific and technical terms that were not being properly explained in the text. The solution was to add a 'Glossary' at the end so that all could be defined. One of the entries in the glossary was, "Elements essential for life" and while I was writing out the list I had a vague feeling that grew stronger as I went on that I had seen that list before.

When I checked I found that most of the names I was writing down were of elements that are strongly matched to their own Bible numeric number. Here was another completely unexpected gem, possibly the most valuable one of all. To include it I had to rewrite the end of the manuscript.

When the manuscript and its index was finished and checked several times the next thing was to find a publisher. I enquired first by email to the people I had previously had contact with in McGraw-Hill. Their answer came back in a few hours, "It is too religious for us but it is something that should be published. Keep trying and good luck!"

The next place to look was the company that publishes, 'Number in Scripture', an American company named Kregel Publications. They have a website which quite clearly says they do not accept unsolicited manuscripts but they referred to another company which they described as a 'pre-editing' company for scriptural manuscripts.

The pre-editing company had contacts with about 50 religious publishers. They offered for a fee to tidy up suitable manuscripts and then offer them to all of their contacts. I sent off the manuscript by email and paid the fee. Their reply was that they would not accept the manuscript because it was not religious enough!?! They would however add information about it to their next newsletter which would be circulated to their list of contacts.

The newsletter brought an offer of a contract from Deep River Books. It was not a first class offer; but it was the only one. I had to contract to buy 1,000 copies of the finished book at the wholesale rate; however, it was an offer and it would get the story printed and on the market. At that time the Australian dollar was worth $US1.20 and for that they would employ a professional editor and typesetter. That work is the expensive part of the publication process and the amount I would have to pay for the thousand books would get that done properly. I accepted their contract and paid the first progress payment.

The title of the book has an interesting story. I submitted about half a dozen suggestions, things like, "Chemical Numerics" or "God's Code" were my favourites. "You Were Designed" was tacked on to the end of the list. It was the one I favoured least but that was the one they chose; it fitted best in the market they operate in.

When the editor started work she obviously would like to have changed the character of the book, she was often asking questions about what she called the, "Journey of discovery" and she several times asked for addition of human interest paragraphs (what I would have described as padding). She had a particular market in mind. I had to trust her expert opinion so I went along with most of her requests and only negotiated on those things that would have caused a distortion of factual information. I found out much later that the market that Deep River Books mainly operate in is something they call 'religious fiction'.

When the book was finally typeset the index had disappeared never to be seen again. Obviously in the minds of the Deep River people it was not to be a reference book any longer. I sometimes wonder whether they actually believed that what I had found was fact or fiction; it is a long way different from what is commonly believed by denominational people.

"You Were Designed – The Code Is In Your Chemicals" was printed and published in late 2014. In early 2015 the 1,000 books arrived from America by sea, they were in 33 boxes on a pallet, the total weight was over 300 kilograms.

I was disappointed by the response of booksellers, none of them were willing to stock it as a regular item. I had a personal contact with an owner of a second-hand book shop, he was willing to give it a try among his stock, at the end of twelve months he gave me back the box with none actually sold. It wasn't just the sellers who were ignoring it, the public had the same opinion. Commercially the project has been a complete failure, the publisher reported sales of 35 books altogether and I was only able to sell about half a dozen.

On the other hand, the book has been read. When they were not selling commercially I donated some to public libraries. There were 26 libraries in South Australia who listed it and after about twelve months an assistant at one of them was able to show me the statistics. Between the 26 of them a book had been borrowed 91 times in that first year. Nancy and I were able to cover most of the libraries in South Australia and the Melbourne, Sydney and Gold Coast metropolitan areas, most of the country areas in western Victoria and some parts of rural New South Wales and north eastern Victoria.

Delivery of books to the Sydney metropolitan area was a particularly memorable occasion. Sydney has a particularly good commuter rail system and road traffic is difficult for interstate visitors. It has over 100 libraries listed and many of them are within walking distance of a railway station. Before we started I located the libraries on a street map and located the most local railway station; I then prepared a schedule of how to get to each station in turn. 100 books plus our personal luggage would have involved us in about $ 800 of excess baggage cost on an airline so we planned to travel by train. Nancy and I loaded our 100 books into three suitcases and drove to Ballarat where we could leave the car with our family who live there. We travelled by train to Melbourne then on an overnight train to Sydney. The train crew had no objection to the three suit cases, there was no extra charge for excess baggage.

Sydney's suburban area is huge. We had found a hotel/motel at Hornsby which looked like it was within walking distance of a railway station and had booked a room there for the week. When we arrived at Sydney Central Station we found a train going on the correct line and it was a trip of 23 kilometres. We had combined our trip with attending a weekend convention at Concord which is closer to the city on the Hornsby line. Concord, a reasonably outer suburb was as big and busy as the centre of Adelaide's CBD. Our first planned delivery trip the next day after the convention was to Richmond which is 60 kilometres from the centre of the city. We went straight there and visited libraries on the way back hopping on and off trains all day. The railway system uses a computer controlled ticketing system in which each person has a plastic card which you place against a terminal each time you enter or leave a station. Amazingly at the end of the day the computer had only charged each of us a bit over $2 for the whole 60 km. and back trip. Apparently it works on a rule that if you spend less than an hour away from the station it is counted as a transfer and not separately charged for. We must have not spent more than an hour at any place so our day's journey was counted as one trip from Hornsby to Hornsby.

For the rest of the week we would initially go to the end of the line then visit libraries on the way back. There was one place where the system enabled trains to get to an outer suburban station by two different lines; on that day we had a loop going out on one line and coming back on the other. We did not quite get to all of the libraries on the list in that week and unfortunately we had a time commitment at the end of it but we gave it a good shot. We were booked at the end of the week to travel back to Melbourne on the day time train. The week had been a great achievement but exhausting. We had to wake up very early in time to get from Hornsby to Sydney Central by 7:30 am but once we were safely on that train I for one just sat for the whole day and watched the scenery slide past at speeds up to 160 kilometres per hour. Nancy still had a little bit more energy left but she didn't do a lot more either.

Later when we were doing a similar activity for the Melbourne metropolitan area its public transport system is marginally less effective than for Sydney and the road traffic marginally less fearsome. We did that by driving from place to place. We didn't have the continual push to be in time to catch a train so it was a bit less personally exhausting but we didn't get to as many libraries in the week either.

I did not keep a count of where all the, "You Were Designed" books were accepted but as a rough estimate I expect that the 26 in South Australia were about a quarter of the total and the demand would have lasted at least a couple of years at close to the original rate; these numbers extrapolate to a total of about 600 to 800 people who have read the book. None of those people will ever look at the Bible in quite the same way again and if it was the key to eternal life for any one of them the whole cost and effort will have been worthwhile for just that one soul.

Chapter 8: Counting on God's Fingers

The whole subject of proof of the numeric code took a bit of a holiday for a couple of years after that but there were things germinating that would lead to the next stage.

In general reading, I had read through the first few chapters of Genesis and noticed the large proportion of the numbers that were divisible by 5 but I did no more about it at the time. A couple of years after that one of the brothers in the Fellowship who knew of my interest in the subject asked if I could write out a simple, concise and accurate explanation of the Bible's numeric code. When I tried I soon found that if it is simple and concise it would not be accurate and if it is simple and accurate it would not be concise.

At about the same time we had a study session in which we looked closely at Revelation chapter 19 and 20. We were able to decide that the passage is describing events that will happen on this physical Earth to people who are some of the descendants of people alive today. Something I particularly noticed was the description of Satan being locked up for 1,000 years and that figure is mentioned six times in a couple of verses. The Bible does not generally use exclamation marks; usually if something is important it is repeated so something that is repeated six times is probably going to be very important indeed!

The scripture as I read it seems to be a warning that Satan will come again after the thousand years possibly on the exact day. I wondered whether it may be a time period in another number base. The only reason we count in tens is because we have four fingers and a thumb on each hand. If we had all been born with a different number of fingers we would use a different base number for our arithmetic. It turns out however that the only number that could be even close is 1024 which could be expressed as 2^{10} or 4^5 or 32^2. In the time sequence the 10^3 thousand will come before the 1024 number so the people of the time will be safe looking out for him on the day the thousand years (10^3) is up. That exercise however, lead me to think about the general subject of arithmetic in other base numbers. We do not know how many fingers God has but we do know that God is not limited by how many fingers we have.

Many years before I had seen a pen and ink sketch of a table relating ages of the patriarchs and their ages when their sons were born. Some years after that I had used the CAD program to draft a more accurately aligned version of that chart which was able to show who of them had face-to-face contact with others older that themselves. I had shown that chart to a group of Sunday School children. Shortly after the previous activity one of the people who had been a child at that time remembered that chart and asked if I still had a copy of it. That had been several computers ago so the chart itself had disappeared into the mists of antiquity but I still had the CAD program in regular use so it would not be a big job to redraft it.

While I was doing the re-drawing I remembered the common appearance of number 5s and added an extra bit to the chart that showed the factors of all the numbers. There was also a significant sprinkling of numbers divisible by 100 which mainly seemed to be matched to the spiritual heroes, such as Enoch and Noah. When I showed the chart to other people they all agreed that it was deliberately made like that but by itself that does not prove anything. It could have been that the writer rounded the numbers to the nearest 5 or even that a fiction writer may have chosen those numbers because he or she just liked them. I was told, "You need to find something else about those numbers if you want to prove they are supernatural".

The numbers are in Genesis chapter 5 and chapter 11 with a couple in the intervening chapters which provide the links between those two lists. From Adam to Abraham's grandson Jacob there are 43 numbers and they have a special feature, they form a discrete group which does not have to be mixed in with the approximately 15,000 other numbers in the Bible.

A test of the gematria as I had done previously for the Third Epistle of John was one possibility. My previous experience suggested that it would be a lot of work and the result for most sentences could easily be inconclusive.

I remembered the previous investigation of the thousand years and the query about the numbers in other bases. It would not be a big task to make a list of these 43 numbers and see what they would look like converted to other bases. I found a big enough piece of paper, wrote the 43 numbers in a column down the left hand side then wrote the numbers in base 4 in a column along-side of them. The chart had enough room for a column for each number base from base 4 to base 16. I tried to keep the columns and rows as straight as possible but after I had corrected some mistakes it was getting pretty messy.

When you do arithmetic with numbers in bases other than base 10 all the arithmetic operations are exactly the same; the numbers are presented using different digits and the carry digits between columns are different but everything else is the same; it just looks different. That means anything that was going to be different about those sums in other bases had to be something to do with the digits.

I was hoping to find a pattern of some sort but I had no idea of what to look for. One of the possibilities I particularly looked for was oblique or horizontal lines of some sort. I can remember expecting that from finding the absence of the number 26 in the chemical elements I may possibly find there would be no '2' digits in the base 13 numbers but that didn't happen. There did appear to be a certain amount of 'clumping' of particular digits in particular parts of the chart. A certain amount of that would be expected. For the base 4 numbers for instance they only have digits for "0" to "3" and the vast excess of fives in the plain language list would mean that a lot of the base 5 numbers should end in zero and for bases which are multiples of 5 there should be many digits "0" and "5". When I looked over the whole chart I got a feeling that there was more to it than those things could explain.

There is however a vast difference between having a vague feeling about some digits on a chart and proving a definite non-random pattern in them!

At first I did a lot of stumbling around in the intellectual darkness and once again I must admit to a bias, I was not even handed but wanted to find a pattern that could be shown to the World. The first test was to use a separate piece of paper for each base number and make an average for each base by counting the total number of all digits on that sheet then dividing by the base number. After that I counted up the total number of appearances of each digit in the 43 words and compared that total with the average. I wrote the numbers down without trying to fit them into columns and without any leading zeros. The most significant digit of each number was discarded because between them they would form a group which would be very obviously non-random. Testing was done on the digits other that the most significant on the expectation that if there was no pattern related to that base all the numbers of digits would be fairly close to that average

For example; the digits for the base 4 numbers are in five columns, the column values are 256, 64, 16, 4 and 1. The patriarch's numbers between 29 and 60 would only occupy the 16s, 4s and 1s columns; the numbers from 65 to 209 would occupy the 64s, 16s, 4s and 1s columns and the larger ones would have a digit in all five columns. Among those numbers (without including most significant digits) there are 46 digit zeros, 24 digit ones, 33 digit twos and 33 digit threes. There are 136 digits altogether and the average is 34 appearances of each digit. In that list the number of zeros is obviously above average and the number of digit ones is below average but the big question is, "Are they far enough away from the average to be significant?"

In sums of this type the quantity that is used to decide probability is the 'standard deviation'. I have as book called, "Facts From Figures" which was first published in 1951. That date is close to the dawn of the silicon age so the book effectively predates the computer age and actually explains how statistics work. That book shows an approximate way of calculating a standard deviation which it calls the, "De Moivre Approximation". A calculation following that instruction showed the standard deviation for the base 4 numbers was 5.05. The result for digit zero then is 2.38 times the standard deviation above the average which corresponds to a chance of one in 111. The result for digit one is 1.98 times the standard deviation below average which corresponds to one chance in 40. These were interesting straws in the wind but given the rough and ready, approximate way they were calculated the surety of the result was still a bit doubtful.

A similar exercise for the numbers expressed in base 5 used digits from "0" to "4" with 47 appearances of digit zero, 25 of digit one, 21 of digit two, 15 of digit three and 9 of digit four. I immediately discounted the result for digit zero, it was almost certainly an artefact of the original fives in the plain language text, but the result for digit four was notable and possibly a provable gem! The total of all of them was 117, the average was 23.4 and the standard deviation by De Moivre Approximation was 4.33. With those figures the result for digit four was 3.3 times the standard deviation below the average and that corresponds to a chance of one in about 3,000. At the time I counted it as a gem, perhaps not quite as hard as a diamond but at least a semi-precious stone.

In the course of time I worked through all the numbers presented in all the bases up to base 16. There was another gem in the form of digit two in the base 7 list and an indication of something notable in digit two in the base 16 list. There were also another 5 results with probability in the range of one in 50 to one in 200 which could be classed as 'straws in the wind' and a host of results less significant than one chance in 40 of which some could be contributors to an overall combination later on.

By the time I had worked through those sums up to that stage, the year 2019 was over half way through. There was a fellowship camp planned for a long weekend in September at Nelson in south western Victoria. I had just enough time to write up an explanation of the experiment and list the results then print off a few copies of it to take to that camp. I knew that some of the people I expected to be there would be willing to read about it and make interested comments. Results were patchy, one was absolutely fascinated by it and others were more doubtful. The overall consensus was that the method of using the numbers themselves as a yardstick to test by was a source of doubt and the appropriate measure may not be the simple average of the numbers of appearances of all the digits.

Chapter 9: The Search For A Yardstick

Whenever an experiment of this type calls for an independent reference the stock answer is, "A random number, or a group of random numbers". It is not that simple; the group of numbers must have certain features.

- It must give every number in the required range an even chance of being picked
- The group must be aperiodic – there must be no detectable patterns
- The selected group must represent the characteristics of the larger group
- When different groups are tried all should give close to the same final result.

This chapter is fairly heavily mathematical. If maths is not your strong point you can skim read to (Kindle 46%) and take up the story from there. The section from there to the end of the chapter is an explanation of why these bits are important. If you read that you will be able to take up the story again in the next chapter.

At first I tried to find a group of 43 numbers that would fit those requirements for tests of all the bases; a sort of set of magic numbers that would be a reference for everything. It was possible to find a set of numbers that could be used for the base four test and it wasn't too bad a fit for base five but results got progressively worse for the higher base numbers.

There was also the question of where to get the random numbers from. One source that has a good reputation in some circles is the least significant digits of a list of telephone numbers. They are a good start but in some cases where the number leads to a group of telephones there can be a series of entries in the list that are all zeros. Results were highly variable and depended a lot on just which set of telephone numbers were used.

There are several websites that offer to provide random numbers but in some of them they don't meet the above list of requirements very well. In an attempt to reduce the variation between individual tests I tested four groups combined; that reduced the variability but I also tried a combination of four groups in which one group had come from telephone numbers and the other three from three different websites; that also became unpredictable. At that stage of the experiment there was almost nothing that was repeatable.

The Facts From Figures book shows how to calculate a 'line of best fit' for the points on a graph. It also describes the actual calculation of a standard deviation figure. The results I was getting could be treated as a graph with the digit number as the 'x' axis and the number of appearances of that digit as the 'y' value. That change did slightly reduce uncertainty and it also pointed a finger at the real cause of the problem.

With a calculated line of best fit and standard deviation, variations in the results of individual tests showed up as changes in the slope of the line. For tests in which the result would be reasonably predictable the line would be close to flat but if the line had a large slope that corresponded to results of lower quality. From that, I soon found a rough tie up between the actual range of numbers used, the size of the base number and the slope of the line.

For all the early tests I had used a set of random numbers ranging from 0 to 1,000 for tests of all the bases. That gave particularly bad results for the base 9 test, the line was a diagonal from a high value for digit zero to almost nothing for digit "8". When I used another group of numbers in the range from 0 to 729 the line was almost flat with a slight upward slope. (729 is 9^3.)

I concentrated on the base 4 sums and spent quite a bit of time trying to work out exactly what a representative sample should look like. At first I reasoned that the numbers from zero to 1023 should be a good start for numbers that would offer a random chance for all digits. When I worked it out however the total of possibilities is a number called 'factorial 1024' which is 10 with about 1,500 zeros after it and if you select groups of 43 out of that you still have about 1,470 zeros and not all of the numbers are equally likely. For the sake of comparison, the total number of sub-atomic particles in the Universe multiplied by the number of pico-seconds between the computed time of the 'big bang' and the present is a number with about 110 digits. It is not possible for a number bigger than that to have any physical meaning.

I drew up a sort of graph with an 'x' axis from 0 to 1024. There are 43 numbers in the test and each would produce 5 digits in the base 4 presentation so the 'y' axis went from 0 to 215. If the 43 numbers were to be allowed to be all the same the result could be a dot on that graph at any position. For each of those sort of dots however there could only be one way that number could be produced. When the 43 numbers have a variety of values the representative dots will be closer to the middle of the graph and are a lot more common because for each one there are many ways each could be produced. For the special case where it is required that all 43 numbers must be different it is possible to draw a boundary line around a shape to represent that condition. For the line on the low side the lowest it ever got was 18 and it ranged from there up to 33. On the high side the highest point was 125 and at some 'x' values it got as low as 82.

If the aim is to select sets of numbers that give every one, an even chance there are two ways in particular to achieve that. Note that these are not groups of random numbers; they are selected to cover the whole range. For all the numbers from 0 to 1023 to be divided into groups of 43 it will require 24 groups.

One way is to use numbers 0 to 42 in a group, 43 to 85 in a second group, 86 to 128 in a third group and continue that pattern for 24 groups. If it must fit exactly to 1023 there will have to be nine groups that each overlap the next group by one number; these can be scattered throughout the 24 groups.

The other way is to make one group of 0, 24, 48, 72, up to the maximum of 990, a second group of 1, 25, 49, 73, up to a maximum of 991 and continue like that for another 22 groups. If the maximum number is to be exactly 1023 there will have to be 9 numbers scattered through the range that are doubled up.

It turns out that when all these numbers are converted to base 4 the two methods form the extremes of a range. The first way produces numbers of digit appearances that are at or close to the extremes of the range for the 'each number once only' shape (18s and 125s). The second way produces numbers in which the appearances of digits are all very close to the average (in range 53 to 56). The suggestion is that groups of random numbers which are specified as 'all numbers different from each other' should tend to form a Gaussian distribution about the average which is 53.75.

For a Gaussian distribution numbers which are more than three times the standard deviation separated from the mean are extremely unlikely with chance in the one in a thousand class. Looking at that the other way round, if we know what the extremes are, then the standard deviation should be approximately one third of that separated from the mean. In the present case the mean is 53.75 and the extremes are 18 and 125 so the one standard deviation range should be about 44 to 70.

The important point about those figures is that for truly random groups of 43 numbers taken from a range of 0 to 1023 and converted into base 4 when a large number of groups are counted there should be 74% of the numbers of each digit in the range from 44 to 70. That exercise had been an incredibly complicated and long winded process but extremely important because it gave me a specification that can be used to test how close to truly random groups of numbers really are. It is a bit uncertain when you attempt to use that specification on individual groups of 43 numbers but it does enable you to get an idea of the quality of a source (such as a website) when you test several groups from the same source.

Up until the time I started that exercise I had done all the calculations by 'pencil and paper' using a calculator for the actual sums. My calculator has some statistical functions on it but I chose not to use them for two reasons. Most basic was that I did not know how to make them work but more importantly if I had pressed all the keys for what I thought was the correct procedure I would get a number on the screen and I would have no idea of whether it was a correct answer or not and I had no way of finding out if the results were wrong.

At first I was still looking for a 'magic' group that would work as a comparison for all the tests. During that exercise I could see that the magic group concept was not workable, that uncertainty would be reduced by using a different set of random numbers for every calculation. It was going to use a lot of repetitive calculations so I set about making an 'Excel' spread sheet program to convert numbers into the required base. From then on I made a point of only using each set of random numbers once and never relying on the result of any one set of numbers.

There were still some loose ends to be resolved. The question of what range to select from reared its ugly head when I tried to adapt the base 4 technique to a base 5 presentation. To have a situation where all digits could be random the numbers would have to run from zero to 3,125 and factorial 3,125 is a number with about 6,000 digits. Obviously that idea was not going to work for all bases.

The patriarch's numbers actually run from the smallest at 29 to the largest at 840. If the test range is the same as that for all bases the most significant column (256s for base 4 or 625s for base 5 etc.) will obviously be very non-random but it is possible in every case to make a random sample by filling all the columns with digits but then only using the three or four less significant columns for the actual comparison. When I tried that on a few different bases it worked very well to sample only 3 columns out of four or five. I actually used numbers in the range from 28 to 841 to make sure that all in the patriarch's range had an even chance. When I had identified that range I used it from then on for tests on all the different bases.

From that time on I was able to do comparative tests on the sources of random numbers. I had made it standard practice by that time to use the combination of four groups of numbers to provide a line of best fit and standard deviation for each test. With that information and the 74% rule it was possible to evaluate the various sources on the basis of good fit to the classical Gaussian distribution. The best were, one whose source of data was an atmospheric noise source and one called, "Calculator Soup" These two both fitted the Gaussian distribution quite well but there were differences between them. For one test I used a combination of two groups from each of those two and the result was not as good as either alone.

When a reliable reference was available its line of best fit could be compared with the patriarch's numbers when they were presented in the same base. The chance of individual digits being random could be found by comparing the number of appearances with the calculated standard deviation.

It had been a tremendously involved and torturous journey but once it was done I had the ability to test the patriarch's numbers in a way that would stand up to any test. Science these days has had to become very legalistic. The risk of being called to account in a court of law hangs over the heads of all investigators at all times; particularly in those cases where someone can see a hope of monetary gain by starting an action. With the evidence I had in my possession I feel confident that I could legally defend these results if ever they were called into question in that way.

Chapter 10: Gems of Proof

There were three separate tests done on the patriarch's base 4 numbers. One test was compared with a set of four groups of numbers from the atmospheric noise source; the second was a test comparing with a set of four groups of numbers from the Calculator Soup website and the third was a test comparing with a set composed of two groups from each of those two sources. They all showed the same trends. The test of the three columns of least significant digits was the one that was not affected by the leading zero problem.

Results for digit "0" were above reference in all three tests with probability figures of one chance in 17, one chance in 22.7 and one chance in 14.7.

Results for digit "1" were below reference to the extent of one chance in 65 for one test and the other two tests gave identical figures of one chance in 24.4.

In all three tests digits "2" and "3" were not significantly different from the reference.

The legally defendable statement is related to the least certain figure in each case. The probability of the result for digit "0" is smaller than one chance in 14.7 and for digit "1" the probability is smaller than one chance in 24.

Those results are useful straws in the wind but not something to get really excited about by themselves. If other results however gave comparable figures they could be contributors to an overall story.

There were also three tests of the base five presentation and as before the tests of the three least significant columns were the ones that gave the clearest results. All tests showed digit "0" vastly above the reference, digit "3" below and digit "4" well below. Digits "1" and "2" were not significantly different from the reference in any of the tests. The result for digit "0" was expected and is assumed to be an artefact of the large proportion of the plain language numbers that are divisible by 5. For digit "3" the results for each of the tests were, one chance in 370, one chance in 58 and one chance in 25. The corresponding figures for digit "4" were one chance in 3,000, one chance in 880 and one chance in 104.

In general use statisticians count any result more certain than one in 20 as being possibly significant and any result more certain that one in 100 as being definitely significant. These probability figures are derived from the difference between, the observed figure for the patriarchs and the figure for the reference, divided by the standard deviation for that test. One chance in 100 corresponds to a difference figure of 2.36 times the standard deviation and one chance in 1,000 corresponds to a difference of just over 3 times the standard deviation. Small changes in the difference figure can correspond to large changes in the probability figure; however, if the probability is smaller than one chance in 100 there are many situations where it matters little how much smaller it is. It is possible to have a situation where one calculation may give a probability figure in the one in thousands range and a matching calculation with different random numbers may give a result of one in low hundreds; these two apparently vastly different figures can confirm and verify each other in certain circumstances.

In these tests we can claim that the result for digit "3" is more certain than one chance in 25 and the result for digit "4" is more certain than one chance in 104. The result for digit "3" is notable, open minded people will take notice and count it as significant but a determined opponent will still express doubt. Digit "4" is a true gem stone, hard and permanent it will not be worn down or broken by even the most single minded opposition.

For the base 6 presentation $6^3 = 216$ and 6^4 is well over 840 so there are only four columns; only the three least significant columns can be used for testing. The results for all the digits except digit "5" were close to the reference. When the patriarch's numbers were compared to random numbers from atmospheric noise the result for digit "5" was a chance of one in 45 but when the same test was done using random numbers from the 'Calculator Soup' website the result was only one chance in 10.7.

For the base 7 presentation $7^3 = 343$ so there will only be four columns; the most significant (343s) will be severely affected by the 'leading zero' factor and the second column (49s) will have seven numbers affected by that factor. In a test comparing the patriarch's numbers with a set of random numbers from the 'Calculator Soup' website, digit "2" was above reference with probability of approximately one chance in 2,500 and digit "6" was below reference with probability of one chance in 570. The rest of the digits gave results that were close enough to the reference to be classed as either not significant or very doubtful.

There was an unfortunate circumstance surrounded an attempt to check those results against a set of random numbers from the atmospheric noise source. When I calculated the line of best fit and standard deviation the groups of numbers had a quite clearly non-Gaussian distribution. The figures indicated by that doubtful reference were one chance in 39 for digit "2" and one chance in 32 for digit "6".

At some time in the future I intend to re-do the request for random numbers from that website. If when I do that the result will back up the figures above from the 'Calculator Soup' website that will make the digit "2" and digit "6" figures into gem stone quality results.

For the base 9 presentation $9^3 = 729$ so the most significant column will only ever contain "0" or "1" and the 81s column in the patriarch's list will have 13 extra zeros more than is due to a random presentation.

Results for the patriarch's numbers expressed in base 9 were. For digit "2" above reference by one chance in 35 when compared to random numbers from the atmospheric noise source and one chance in 21 when compared to 'Calculator Soup' numbers. For digit "4" below reference by one chance in 308 compared to atmospheric noise and one chance in 73 compared to 'Calculator Soup' numbers. There was also a marginally significant result below reference for digit "6". All the other digits were close to their reference.

The base 4, base 5, base 6, base 7 and base 9 presentations were the only ones that showed significant relationships in the preliminary tests. Presentations in the other base numbers have not yet been tested against random number groups.

The original purpose of this exercise was to test numbers listed in Genesis chapters 5 to 11 and identify whether any below-the-surface matching exists. This was to test and verify those numbers as a non-random series of numbers divisible by five and in some cases divisible by 100. What has been found is an intricate web of highly significant matches of interrelated components of those numbers that could not possibly have happened by chance.

The large proportion of the plain language numbers that are divisible by five produces artefacts in these calculations; those artefacts can be identified and it is demonstrated that the significant matching discovered in these calculations is not due to artefacts of that plain language relationship.

It is also noteworthy that the matching (or negative matching in some cases) between base numbers and digits is in accordance with the concepts of the Bible numeric code which were defined by non-mathematicians about 120 years ago before the calculating techniques used in this book were widely used for scientific investigation.

When I had worked through the calculations to that stage I felt that it was time to start looking for other people who may be interested in the subject. I wrote up the booklet that is reprinted in the next chapter and passed a few copies around to others in the fellowship who I thought might be able to use the information. The booklet was actually written in two stages; the base 4 and base 5 calculations were the first stage which ended with a calculation that the combined result of those two had one chance in 1,001 of being a random result. I thought that was good enough to validate the significance of the number 5s that I had found in the original plain language text.

The final few pages referring to bases 6, 7 and 9 were added later.

Chapter 11: The Patriarch's Numbers

The following is the text of a booklet prepared as an initial statement of the calculations. A small number of copies were made and given to some of my closest associates for assessment purposes. It was prepared in two stages, the first part up to the end of the section entitled "Q.E.D." was the subject as developed to 15 – 4 – 2020 and the final part added the developments to end of June 2020. The purpose of its addition here is to give you opportunity to check my calculations if you feel that is necessary. The original booklet was 65 pages of A5 printing with only one illustration; significant changes have been necessary to adapt it for the E-book presentation.

THE QUESTION?

The book of Genesis has accounts of the lives of particular people for about the first two and a half thousand years since the dawn of recorded history. There is a fairly detailed account of one day in the lives of Adam and Eve and a chapter about their sons then for the following five generations the only things recorded are their name, how old they were when their son was born and how long they lived after that time. The book records the fact that they had other children as well but apart from that nothing else about them is recorded. No record of who their wives were or the names and ages of the other children or how they made their living; nothing about what they thought or said and not even any record of whether God approved of what they did or not. There is just a list of names and numbers and that is all.

After that came E'noch; Very little more is said about him except that he, "Walked with God and he was not, for God took him". Much later in the New Testament epistles E'noch is referred to that he had this testimony, "He pleased God".

After E'noch there was another two generations of just the names and numbers and then Noah. There are several chapters telling the famous story of Noah, how he was warned by God of a coming flood and he and his sons built an ark to preserve their family and samples of the animals while everything around them was drowned in the flood.

After the story of Noah and his sons there is another eight generations for which very little except names and numbers is recorded then Abram whose name was changed to Abraham. From the time of Abraham onwards the story is much more detailed. The numbers continue until the generation of Jacob, Abraham's grandson. Jacob's age when his sons were born is not recorded. In that list there are 22 generations spanning over 2,000 years and a total of 43 numbers. There is a great glaring question about that story.

WHY?

Why should there be such detail about names and numbers and almost nothing else about one third of the time period from the dawn of recorded history until now. Is there a secret code or message in the names or the numbers or both?

THE PRIMARY DATA.

In this list the event is identified and immediately following it there is a number which is the number of years it occupied then after the equal sign there are the factors of that number expressed in prime numbers

Adam's age when Seth born 130 years = $2 \times 5 \times 13$
Adam lived after Seth born 800 years = $2^5 \times 5^2$

Seth's age when Enos born 105 years = $3 \times 5 \times 7$
Seth lived after Enos born 807 years = 3×269

Enos' age when Ca-i'nan born 90 years = $2 \times 3^2 \times 5$
Enos lived after Ca-i'nan born 815 years = 5×163

Ca-i'nan's age when Ma-ha'la-le-el born 70 years = $2 \times 5 \times 7$
Ca-i'nan lived after Ma-ha'la-le-el born 840 years = $2^3 \times 3 \times 5 \times 7$

Ma-ha'la-le-el's age when Jared born 65 years = 5×13
Ma-ha'la-le-el lived after Jared born 830 years = $2 \times 5 \times 83$

Jared's age when E'noch born 162 years = 2×3^4
Jared lived after E'noch born 800 years = $2^5 \times 5^2$

E'noch's age when Me-thu'se-lah born 65 years = 5×13
E'noch lived after Me-thu'se-lah born 300 years = $2^2 \times 3 \times 5^2$

Me-thu'se-lah's age when La'mech born 187 years = 11×17
Me-thu'se-lah lived after La'mech born 782 years = 2×391

La'mech's age when No'ah born 182 years = $2 \times 7 \times 13$

La'mech lived after No'ah born 595 years = 5 x 7 x 17

No'ah's age when Shem born 500 years = 2^2 x 5^3
No'ah lived after Shem born 450 years = 2 x 3^2 x 5^2

Shem's age when Ar-phax'ad born 100 years = 2^2 x 5^2
Shem lived after Ar-phax'ad born 500 years = 2^2 x 5^3

Ar-phax'ad age when Sa'lah born 35 years = 5 x 7
Ar-phax'ad lived after Sa'lah born 403 years = prime
number

Sa'lah's age when E'ber born 30 years = 2 x 3 x 5
Salah lived after E'ber born 403 years = prime number

E'ber's age when Pe'leg born 34 years = 2 x 17
E'ber lived after Pe'leg born 430 years = 2 x 5 x 43

Pe'leg;s age when Re'u born 30 years = 2 x 3 x 5
Pe'leg lived after Re'u born 209 years = 11 x 19

Re'u's age when Se'rug born 32 years = 2^5
Re'u lived after Se'rug born 207 years = 3^2 x 23

Se'rug's age when Na'hor born 30 years = 2 x 3 x 5
Se'rug lived after Na'hor born 200 years = 2^3 x 5^2

Na'hor's age when Te'rah born 29 years = prime
number
Na'hor lived after Te'rah born 119 years = 7 x 17

Te'rah's age when Abraham born 70 years = 2 x 5 x 7
Te'rah lived after Abraham born 135 years = 3^3 x 5

Abraham's age when I'saac born 100 years = 2^2 x 5^2
Abraham lived after I'saac born 75 years = 3 x 5^2

I'saac's age when Jacob born 60 years = $2^2 \times 3 \times 5$
I'saac lived after Jacob born 120 = $2^3 \times 3 \times 5$

Jacob lived 147 years = 3×7^2

Jacob's age when his sons were born is not recorded.

Looking at the numbers themselves reveals very little in the way of hidden or secret codes. Investigators have laid out charts of the numbers and shown that while Adam lived all the generations from Seth to Lamech were born and that all down to Lamech could talk face to face with Adam. Then Noah's son Shem could talk face to face with Lamech and Shem was still alive when Abram was born so the story of Adam and Eve in the garden was only third hand information even at the time of Abraham.

The other thing the numbers themselves reveal is the gradual drift from the 800 to 900 year lifespans that were normal at first down to the less than 200 years that applied to Abraham and his descendants. That drift has continued and is still happening today.

There is a point to be noted about this list of ages; it is the list of numbers actually recorded in Genesis chapter 5 and chapter 11. For some cases it is possible to compute other likely combinations, but for the purpose of defining a possible coded message the first trial must be with the numbers as written.

THE FACTORS

In the absence of a definite relationship we can expect that for a random group of numbers one half of them will be divisible by two, one third of them divisible by three and so on. For a group of 43 numbers random chance would expect that about 8 or 9 of them would be divisible by 5 and only one or two divisible by 100; for this group there are 28 divisible by 5 and 8 are divisible by 100. That is a very obviously non-random event; it has about one chance in 30,000,000 of happening by accident. It was very quickly pointed out to me however that it is no evidence of any supernatural cause, it certainly was caused by something but it may have been no more than the original writer rounding the numbers to the nearest 5 or 10 or even a fiction writer choosing those numbers for the story. The message I was given was that if I could find another less easily fabricated relationship in those numbers that would be evidence of something supernatural and may even validate the association with the factor 5.

AND NOW, FOR SOMETHING COMPLETELY DIFFERENT

Many years ago I was reading in the book of Revelation chapter 20 about the events that will happen when Jesus Christ returns. Satan will be locked up and the time period of one thousand years is repeated six times in a few verses. The Bible does not generally use exclamation marks to draw attention to particular points but when things are important they are repeated.

An example is the conversation between Jesus and Nicodemus reported in chapter 3 of the gospel of John. Jesus said, "Verily, verily you must be born again" and the whole statement is itself repeated in greater detail a couple of verses later.

When a statement is repeated six times in a few verses it must be very important! There will need to be someone, or a series of people, who keep track of the days passing and will be able to identify to the nearest day when that thousand years is finishing. When Satan re-appears he will not be the horrible monster that is commonly portrayed, he will possibly be a handsome debonair business leader with some very persuasive new ideas.

Another factor may be important. Is the statement, "A thousand years" signifying the 10 cubed number that we use or could it be a number close to that from another base. The numbering system we use is technically described as 'positional notation base 10'. We use 10 because we have four fingers and a thumb on each hand and little children first learn counting using their fingers. It is technically possible however to use any number as the base, the digits in each column are different and the carry digits from column to column are different but all the arithmetic operations work exactly the same way.

For humans, doing arithmetic in bases we are not familiar with, is laborious and difficult. We continually have to keep translating back to the base we know. For God, however, He is intellectually powerful enough to work in any base He chooses and could even switch bases halfway through the sum if He wanted to.

It turns out that the only other number that is anywhere close to a thousand is 1,024 which could be either 2^{10} or 4^5 or 32^2. The next nearest is 31^2 which is 961; further out from that are 1,296 which is 6^4, 900 which is 30^2 and 729 which is 9^3. I haven't investigated this any further, it is probably not a serious possibility but what it did do was opened up the train of thought as a possibility in other directions.

When I thought about the Patriarchs numbers I remembered having thought previously about other bases and wondered what effect that would have. I found a big sheet of paper and wrote all the Patriarchs numbers down the left hand side then across the top made a column for base 4, a column for base 5 and so on up to base 16 then started filling in the columns. I'm not sure what I hoped to find but I was looking for patterns of some sort. There wasn't much that really showed in any definite way but as I looked more closely at individual columns I could see that some digits were a lot more common than others.

The next step was to get an individual piece of paper for each base number, write out the numbers converted to that base and actually count the digits in detail. The expectation was that for most of the digits the total number should be about the same for all except the most significant digit of each number. There would of course be a random variation about that common average but that was where the mathematics started to get heavy. There turned out to be quite substantial variations in some cases but the question was how much was random and how much was a significant pointer to a real pattern?

If you are someone who doesn't think easily in numbers or finds maths hard and confusing you can follow the thread of the story by jumping from here to, "The search for a reliable reference" at (Kindle 63%) and then to, "Results of the base 4 calculations" at (Kindle 75%), go on to read the first few paragraphs at the start of the, "Base 5 calculations" on the next page then read from, "Round up" at (Kindle 79%) onwards.

THE NORMAL (GAUSSIAN) DISTRIBUTION

I have a book about statistical methods called, "Facts From Figures" which was first published in 1951; my copy was printed in 1962. It is highly valuable because it was written in the era before computers took over the number crunching and it gives understanding of the principles not just some step-by-step instructions. That book devotes a whole chapter to, "The Normal Distribution".

In a sense The Normal Distribution could be described as a sort of graph or it could also be thought of as a function and a set of rules for making a whole series of graphs all with the same general shape. It is often called, "The bell shaped curve". This diagram which is presented as landscape looked at from the right hand side shows the shape of a typical 'Normal Distribution' curve.

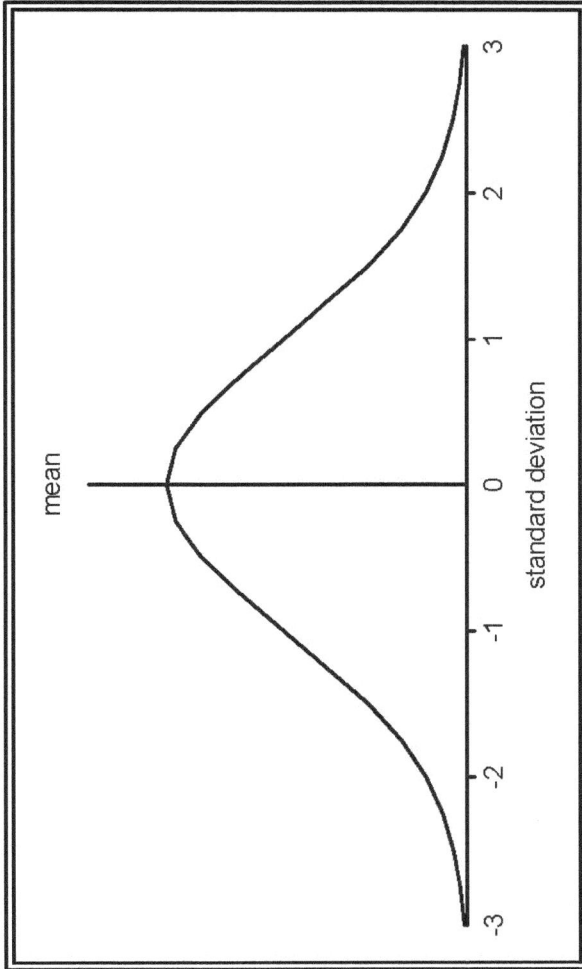

Typical shape of a 'normal distribution' curve.

Carl Friedrich Gauss was a brilliant German mathematician and astronomer who lived about 200 years ago and advanced the theoretical basis of mathematics in many different directions. The function that bears his name is only one of many things he turned his attention to. In essence the normal distribution describes the combined behaviour of large numbers of unrelated events or processes. It describes the sound of wind, waterfalls and rain on an iron roof. It gives predictions about what large numbers of people will do under certain conditions, indicates when customers will walk through your shop door and accounts for measurement errors in scientific experiments. In that role it has become the touchstone and universal arbiter of truth where it occupies a central role in the modern science of probability theory.

If a particular graph of probability is truly random the shape of its curve can be exactly specified with two figures. One is the central point called the 'mean' which for a truly random graph is the point of highest probability; the other is the 'standard deviation' which is a measure of how wide the graph is. The probability figure for a particular point on the graph can be exactly defined by the number of times its position is bigger or smaller than the standard deviation.

OUTLINE OF A FIRST EXPERIMENT

For each of the base numbers between 4 and 16 a list was made of the 43 original numbers expressed in that base and the number of appearances of each digit was counted. For a random result the expectation for most digits is that the total number of appearances will be approximately equally divided between the relevant digits. The most significant digit of each number does not form a random group; the appearances are crowded towards the lower digits but there are no zeros at all in that group. For this test of each base number the most significant digit of each individual number was not counted.

This experiment was to test for non-random relationships between the base numbers and the digits of each number expressed in that base.

A figure for the expected mean was calculated by dividing the total of appearances of all digits (except for the most significant) by the number of digits relevant to that base number.

A figure for the expected standard deviation was calculated using the "De Moivre Approximation" (instructions from the, 'Facts From Figures' book) and the probability of each result being random could be derived from the standard shape of the Gaussian distribution by comparison with that standard deviation figure. In the results listed below a figure of one chance in 1,000 indicates 99.9% certainty that the result is due to a real cause-and-effect relationship whereas a result expressed as one chance in less than 10 indicates that it is quite likely to be accidental with no real relationship between the numbers in the test.

The formula for the "De Moivre Approximation" is

$$(sigma) = \sqrt{(x.y.n)}$$

In this formula:-

(sigma) is the symbol for standard deviation,
x is for the major factor of the probability fraction,
y is for the minor factor of the probability fraction,
n is the total number of samples in that test.

SUMMARY OF EARLY RESULTS

In the tests for base 5, base 10 and base 15 there were a number of highly significant results which could be shown to be artefacts of the significant result for the number 5 in the original text. These were ignored for the same reason as the original result was objected to.

After the most significant digits, these artefacts and the low probability random noise results were removed the following significant results remained. Note that none of these can be explained by random chance or by any other natural cause.

In the result for the base 4 test there were a total of 130 digits of which 45 were digit "0". The mean of these is 32.5 and there is one chance in 180 of this result being a random event.

In the result for the base 5 test there were a total of 113 digits of which 9 were digit "4". The mean is 22.6. This result for digit "4" has one chance in approx. 1,850 and is highly indicative of a supernatural negative relationship between number 4 and number 5 (the Grace of God).

In the result for the base 6 test there were a total of 95 digits; the mean is 15.83 and all except digit "4" gave results well within the range for random events. There were 22 appearances of digit "4"; this result had a chance of one in 25; in context of a strong negative relationship between the number 4 and the number 5 may indicate a tendency for number 4 and number 6 to be positively associated.

In the result for the base 7 test there were a total of 90 digits; the mean is 12.86. There were 24 appearances of digit "2"; this indicates one chance in 2,200 of it being a random event.

In the result for the base 9 test there were a total of 78 digits and the mean is 8.667. there were 15 appearances of digit "2" which corresponds to a chance of one in 100.

In the result for the base 10 (decimal system) test there were 68 digits in total; mean of the ten digits is 6.8 and apart from digit "0" the most significant was the result for digit "6" which only had one appearance. This corresponds to a chance of one in 100.

For the base numbers between 11 and 16 the sample size is small and spread between too many digits to be significant in most cases however some possibly significant results were found.

THE SEARCH FOR A RELIABLE REFERENCE

For all its impressive probability figures that first simple result was still open to doubt. One objection is that there is no surety that the simple average of the number of appearances of each digit is in fact the correct figure to measure against; another stems from the use of an approximation for the standard deviation when an actual calculation may give a very different figure; in the range of probabilities in question the figure expressed as one chance in (some number) is highly dependent on the exact value of the standard deviation calculated. Finally, the simple deletion of the most significant digit introduces another uncertainty into the calculations.

A much more certain result could be gained by finding another group of numbers (or many other groups) with general characteristics close to those of the Patriarchs list but not related to anything supernatural then doing actual calculations on those numbers and make a comparison with the Patriarchs list. A list of random numbers with a calculated line of best fit and a standard deviation figure actually calculated from that line would give a much more reliable comparison.

The list cannot be just any old list of numbers; it should have certain properties such as:-

- It should be a list of 43 numbers which are representative of the larger group
- It should cover the whole range of the Patriarchs list and give an equal chance of selection to each of the numbers in that range
- It should be aperiodic – that means there should be no definable repetitive patterns within the list

It actually took some considerable time and quite a lot of trials of different lists to find some sets of numbers that met that specification.

One of the first lessons I learnt is that a single list of numbers by itself leading to a single set of figures for appearance of digits is almost useless on its own. The numbers required must come from the average of several lists combined. I settled on using groups of four lists combined and averaged.

At first I tried to find a single set of lists that would somehow magically be a good comparison for all the tests in every base column; it worked for a few bases but was wildly out in others.

The range of numbers being tested caused some extra work. For base 4 it was possible to make the range from 0 to 1023 and all digits could be random however when the same principle was applied to base 5 the numbers would have to go from 0 to 3124. For lists of numbers to 1023 the total number of possibilities is factorial 1023 divided by factorial 43 and not all possibilities are equally likely. Factorials of big numbers are nasty animals, this one is a number with about 1,470 digits and the one for base 5 has about 6,000 digits and with that range of numbers the first digit of each of the Patriarchs numbers would either be 0 or 1.

The actual range of the Patriarchs numbers is 29 to 840 and my final position was to abandon the attempt to make the first digit random and use the range 28 to 841 for all the base numbers.

I had done all the early calculations by hand using only a small group of numbers for the reference list. When it became obvious that I would need many lists all with different numbers I took the plunge and attempted a spread sheet program to handle the translation of numbers into another base. That had the side effect of ending consideration of the non-random most significant digit; the program automatically filled in a zero for all in the low end of the range. With that program it was possible to calculate using only the four or three columns of least significant digits to avoid the effect of the non-random most significant digit.

THE SPREADSHEET CALCULATIONS

In the following pages there is an example of how the random base 10 numbers were translated into other bases. The following illustrations are of printouts from an Excel file. The full Excel calculation was for 43 lines of numbers, only 15 are shown in these illustrations for the sake of clarity. The formula for each column of row 2 is:-

For 'Spread Sheet Display, Left Hand Side'

Column A < The name of the calculation >

Column B < The base 10 number to be translated >

Column C < =B2/256 >

Column D < =B2-(K2*256) >

For 'Spread sheet display, inner left'

Column D

Column E < =D2/64 >

Column F < =D2-(L2*64) >

Column G < =F2/16 >

For 'Spread sheet display, inner right'

Column G

Column H < =F2-(M2*16) >

Column I < =H2/4 >

Column J < =H2-(N2*4) >

For 'Spread sheet display, results'

Column K < =INT(C2) >

Column L < =INT(E2) >

Column M < =INT(G2) >

Column N < =INT(I2) >

Column O < =H2-(N2*4) >

A	B	C	D
Base 4	Decimal	Div by 256	remain
Template	1	0.003906	1
	2	0.007813	2
	3	0.011719	3
	4	0.015625	4
	5	0.019531	5
	15	0.058594	15
	16	0.0625	16
	17	0.066406	17
	63	0.246094	63
	64	0.25	64
	255	0.996094	255
	256	1	0
	257	1.003906	1
	322	1.257813	66

Spread sheet display, left hand side.

D	E	F	G
remain	Div by 64	remain	Div by 16
1	0.015625	1	0.0625
2	0.03125	2	0.125
3	0.046875	3	0.1875
4	0.0625	4	0.25
5	0.078125	5	0.3125
15	0.234375	15	0.9375
16	0.25	16	1
17	0.265625	17	1.0625
63	0.984375	63	3.9375
64	1	0	0
255	3.984375	63	3.9375
0	0	0	0
1	0.015625	1	0.0625
66	1.03125	2	0.125

Spread sheet display, inner left.

G	H	I	J
Div by 16	remain	Div by 4	remain
0.0625	1	0.25	1
0.125	2	0.5	2
0.1875	3	0.75	3
0.25	4	1	0
0.3125	5	1.25	1
0.9375	15	3.75	3
1	0	0	0
1.0625	1	0.25	1
3.9375	15	3.75	3
0	0	0	0
3.9375	15	3.75	3
0	0	0	0
0.0625	1	0.25	1
0.125	2	0.5	2

Spread sheet display, inner right.

K	L	M	N	O
256s	64s	16s	4s	1s
0	0	0	0	1
0	0	0	0	2
0	0	0	0	3
0	0	0	1	0
0	0	0	1	1
0	0	0	3	3
0	0	1	0	0
0	0	1	0	1
0	0	3	3	3
0	1	0	0	0
0	3	3	3	3
1	0	0	0	0
1	0	0	0	1
1	1	0	0	2

Spread sheet display, results.

SOURCES OF THE NUMBERS

The source of the lists was a problem. At first I purposely selected four lists from sources as diverse as possible but I soon found that not all sources are truly random and that blunted the direction of the calculations. I used a source from the least significant digits of a list of private telephone numbers but that turned out to be loaded with extra 1s and zeros. Later I used four sources from the internet but results were patchy. After that I tried collecting four lists from each of those individual sources and that was illuminating. Not all sources of so called random numbers are truly random. Finally, I settled on two sources; one was the website Random.org whose numbers are sourced from atmospheric noise; the other was the website Calculator Soup which was the best of the digital program sources.

AN EXAMPLE OF THE LINE OF BEST FIT CALCULATION

Four groups of random numbers from the 'Random.org' (atmospheric noise) website were converted to base 4 using the Excel program. The numbers shown in this table are the total number of appearances of the relevant digit in all five of the 'results' columns (column K to column O).

Digit	Group 1.1	Group 2.1	Group 3.1	29 to 840
"0"	46	55	63	58
"1"	54	58	61	50
"2"	66	62	45	51
"3"	49	40	46	56

The raw data

The total number of times the relevant digit appeared in any of the five columns in the spread sheet calculation for each group.

The 'Facts From Figures' book describes a line of best fit as the straight line on a graph which requires the least total adjustment of all the data points in the condition in which the adjustment figures are squared. The theory is that when data points on a graph are scattered about an average line an adjustment or correction figure can be calculated for each point. Each of those adjustment figures is squared and a total of all the squares is calculated. The line is then adjusted for position and slope to make that total of squares as small as possible.

The book shows three separate calculations for a line of best fit. The most basic is a simple step-by-step process that a reader can easily check that it is in fact giving the intended result. There are then two other procedures which are less intuitive but it is demonstrated that they both give the same result with the same set of data points. The procedure that I have used is the least intuitive but the most versatile; it is based on deriving two separate equations for each data point.

In contrast to the common situation for these equations the "Y" and "X" values are known. The "X" value is the number of the digit and the "Y" value is the total number of times that digit appears in any of the "results' columns of each of the spread sheet calculations. The unknowns to be calculated are the values for "c" and "m". When the "m" term is evaluated it will be the slope of the line of best fit and the "c" term will be the Y axis intercept ("Y" value when "X" is zero). In the following tables there is an individual pair of equations for each of the 16 figures above.

One of the equations is the standard equation of a straight line; Y = mx + c. In the other equation each of those terms individually is multiplied by the "X" value to give XY = X(mx) + Xc. In use each data point is given an instance of each equation in which the "X" and "Y" terms are replaced by the appropriate numbers then all the individual terms of each equation are totalled. The two totalled equations can then be treated as simultaneous equations to isolate the value of either the "m" or "c" term whichever is most convenient.

The calculation is split over three sheets to fit into the display of the Kindle reader. The first sheet deals with numbers from the top two lines of the 'Raw Data' panel, the second sheet deals with the numbers in the bottom two lines of the 'Raw Data' panel and the third sheet show how these individual sums are combined in the simultaneous equation to reveal the final result.

Digit	Y = mx + c	XY = X(mx) + Xc
"0"	46 = 0 + c	0 = 0*0 + 0
	55 = 0 + c	0 = 0*0 + 0
	63 = 0 + c	0 = 0*0 + 0
	58 = 0 + c	0 = 0*0 + 0
	222 = 0 + 4c	0 = 0*0 + 0
"1"	54 = m + c	54 = m + c
	58 = m + c	58 = m + c
	61 = m + c	61 = m + c
	50 = m + c	50 = m + c
	223 = 4m + 4c	223 = 4m + 4c

Line of best fit   sheet 1 of 3

Digit	Y = mx + c	XY = X(mX) + Xc
"2"	66 = 2m + c	132 = 4m + 2c
	62 = 2m + c	124 = 4m + 2c
	45 = 2m + c	90 = 4m + 2c
	51 = 2m + c	102 = 4m + 2c
	224 = 8m + 4c	448 = 16m + 8c
"3"	49 = 3m + c	147 = 9m + 3c
	40 = 3m + c	120 = 9m + 3c
	46 = 3m + c	138 = 9m + 3c
	56 = 3m + c	168 = 9m + 3c
	191 = 12m + 4c	573 = 36m + 12c

Line of best fit   sheet 2 of 3

```
Digit     Subtotals

"0"  222 = 0 + 4c          0 = 0*0 + 0

"1"  223 = 4m + 4c        223 = 4m + 4c

"2"  224 = 8m + 4c        448 = 16m + 8c

"3"  191 = 12m + 4c       573 = 36m + 12c
     _____      _____
        860 = 24m + 16c    1244 = 56m + 24c
```

A simultaneous equation is formed by multiplying the left hand equation by 1.5.

$$1244 = 56m + 24c$$
$$- (1290 = 36m + 24c)$$

$$-46 = 20m \qquad\qquad m = -2.3$$

$$56m = -128.8$$
$$24c = 1244 + 128.8 \qquad\qquad c = 57.2$$

The equation of the line of best fit is

$$Y = 57.2 - 2.3X$$

Line of best fit   sheet 3 of 3

A similar calculation will be needed for the four column test (Ignoring 256s column) and for the three column test (Ignoring 256s and 64s columns).

For the base 5 investigation the column values are 625, 125, 25, 5 and 1; the digits range from "0" to"4" and the number of lines of equations is 20 instead of 16.

For the base 6 investigation only four columns will be used, the values will be 216, 36, 6 and 1; the digits will range from "0' to "5" and the number of lines of equations will be 24.

EXAMPLE OF A STANDARD DEVIATION CALCULATION

After the line of best fit is calculated it is used to calculate a reference figure (shown in the "Ref." columns of the following two sheets) for each digit. The Standard Deviation calculation uses the differences (shown in the "Diff." columns of the following two sheets) between the 16 individual figures above and that reference. Each difference figure is squared, the squares are averaged and the Standard Deviation is the square root of that average of squares figure. The following three sheets of illustration show how that works in practice.

Digit	Ref.	Appearances	Diff.	Squared
"0"	57.2	46	11.2	125.44
		55	2.2	4.84
		63	5.8	33.64
		58	0.8	0.64
				164.56
"1"	54.9	54	0.9	0.81
		58	3.1	9.61
		61	6.1	37.21
		50	4.9	24.01
				71.64

Example of a Standard Deviation calculation

sheet 1 of 3

Digit	Ref.	Appearances	Diff.	Squared
"2"	52.6	66	13.4	179.56
		62	9.4	88.36
		45	7.6	57.76
		51	1.6	2.56
				328.24
"3"	50.3	49	1.3	1.69
		40	10.3	106.09
		46	4.3	18.49
		56	5.7	32.49
				158.76

Example of a Standard Deviation calculation

sheet 2 of 3

The figure 0.6745 has been calculated by mathematicians. In a perfect Normal Distribution half of the data points (figures in the "Diff." columns in the above two sheets) will be closer to the mean than 0.6745 times the Standard Deviation. The adjustment figure calculated is a guide to the reliability of the reference as a representative of a much larger group of random numbers. Small discrepancies only have a minor effect on the final probability figure; in this series where the base 4 calculations have 16 data points altogether if the (sigma x 0.6745) figure is seven or nine instead of eight that is unlikely to change the overall conclusion but if the result of that step in the calculation was a number two or three separated from the mid-point that would cast doubt on the randomness of the figures originally supplied by the websites.

Digit	Subtotals
"0"	164.56
"1"	71.64
"2"	328.24
"3"	156.76
Total	723.2
Divide by 16	45.2
Square root	6.723

The unadjusted Standard Deviation is 6.72

Adjustment for Gaussian Distribution

6.723 x 0.6745 = 4.5347

There are seven data points that have smaller differences than 4.5; the eighth is 4.9 and the ninth is 5.7.

The average between these two is 5.3.

6.723 x 5.3 / 4.5347 = 7.8576

The adjusted standard deviation is 7.86.

Example of a
Standard Deviation calculation sheet 3 of 3

In the, "Comparison with the Patriarchs" section in the following illustration the reference figure is from the line of best fit; the figures in the, 'Patriarch' column are the actual numbers of times each digit appears in the list of Patriarchs expressed in that base and the figure in the, "Significance" column is obtained by dividing the difference figure by the Standard Deviation calculated above. The symbol, "sigma" is the generally used symbol for, "Standard Deviation".

Note that in this case the difference figures, recorded in the "Diff." column of the following illustration, are the difference between the "Patriarchs" figure and the reference; they are not related to the differences between the reference and the number of appearances of each digit of random numbers used above for the calculation of a standard deviation figure.

Digit Ref.   Patriarch   Diff.   Significance

"0"   57.2   82   24.8 3.16σ above ref

"1"   54.9   45   9.9 1.26σ below ref.

"2"   52.6   44   8.6 1.09σ below ref.

"3"   50.3   44   6.3 $<$ one σ from ref.

The result for digit "0" is almost certainly due to the leading zero factor so can be ignored.

The result for digit "1" corresponds to a chance of one in 9.6 which is not generally regarded as significant.

The results for digits "2" and "3" are definitely not significant.

Base 4, atmos.

Patriarchs comparison, 5 column

OTHER CALCULATIONS FOR BASE 4

For the base 4 test of five columns shown in detail in the previous section the effect of the non-random leading zero was quite apparent and was substantial enough to render the calculation of doubtful value. The corresponding calculation of four columns (256s column ignored) was also affected by the same leading zero factor.

In this test of three columns, which are 16s, 4s and units, from the same four groups of random numbers derived from atmospheric noise the same steps of calculation are used.

Digit	Group 1.1	Group 2.1	Group 3.1	29 to 840
"0"	29	35	36	30
"1"	36	34	38	31
"2"	34	34	22	31
"3"	30	26	33	37

For these groups of numbers:-

The equation of the line of best fit is

$$Y = 33.378 - 0.75X$$

The standard deviation is   3.52

Base 4 atmos. random numbers, 3 columns,

In this sheet the standard deviation is the 'adjusted' figure; the unadjusted figure is 4.01 and there are nine numbers with differences smaller than (4.01 x 0.6745). Use of the unadjusted figure would cause the results in the following chart to be slightly less significant. In this comparison which is substantially free of the leading zero function the result for digit "1" is most likely to be mathematically significant and the result for digit zero is also worth noting for future reference.

Digit	Ref.	Patriarch	Diff.	Significance
"0"	33.378	39	5.622	1.60 σ above ref.
"1"	32.628	25	7.628	2.17 σ below ref.
"2"	31.878	34	2.122	< one σ from ref.
"3"	31.128	31	0.128	< one σ from ref.

The result for digit "1" corresponds to one chance in 65 which is probably significant.

The result for digit "0" corresponds to one chance in 17 which is possibly not significant but may be a contributor to the result of another test.

The results for digits "2" and "3" are not significant.

Base 4 atmos.
Patriarchs correspondence, 3 column.

In an exactly similar set of calculations to all of the above; four groups of numbers sourced from the Calculator Soup digital program were translated into base 4 presentation. This first test shown in the following two illustrations used all five columns from the Excel files.

Digit	C Soup	Group 1	Group 2	Group 3
"0"	63	58	56	69
"1"	52	55	57	48
"2"	50	47	54	58
"3"	50	55	48	40

For these groups of numbers

The equation of the line of best fit is

$$Y = 59.825 - 4.05X$$

The Standard Deviation is 4.85

Base 4 soup

random numbers, 5 columns

Digit	Ref.	Patriarch	Diff.	Significance
"0"	59.825	82	22.175	4.57 σ above ref.
"1"	55.775	45	10.775	2.22 σ below ref.
"2"	51.725	44	7.725	1.60 σ below ref.
"3"	47.675	44	3.675	< one σ from ref.

The result for digit "0" is almost certainly an artefact of the non-random leading zeros in the 256s columns.

The result for digit "1" corresponds to one chance in 75 and may be an artefact of the large slope (-4.05X) of the line of best fit.

The result for digit "2" corresponds to one chance in 17 so is of doubtful significance and the result for digit "3" is definitely not significant.

Base 4 soup, Patriarchs comparison 5 column

In the above test using digits from all five columns the results are obviously severely affected by the non-random nature (almost all zeros or ones) of the 256s column in each group. In the Patriarchs list there are eight numbers less than 64 and a further 10 which are less than 128 so the non-random leading digit function affects both the digit "0" and digit '1" figures of the four column test as well. Because of that the four column test has not been done.

The test shown in the following two illustrations used three columns (16s, 4s and units) of the same numbers from the Calculator Soup digital program as were used for the five column test. In this trial the mid-point of the differences list matched with the (sigma x 0.6745) number so no adjustment of standard deviation is needed.

Digit	C Soup	Group 1	Group 2	Group 3
"0"	34	33	32	40
"1"	28	29	31	25
"2"	27	31	34	35
"3"	40	36	32	29

For these groups of numbers

The line of best fit is $Y = 31.95 + 0.2X$

The Standard Deviation is   4.11

Base 4, soup, random numbers 3 column

This comparison is substantially free of the effect of the non-random leading digits and shows two results which are probably significant in the mathematical sense. If these statistics were in a factory quality control activity the procedure would be to take another set of samples and repeat the test however in this case we only have one set of Patriarch's numbers to work from.

Digit	Ref.	Patriarchs	Diff.	Significance
"0"	31.95	39	7.05	1.72σ above ref.
"1"	32.15	25	7.15	1.74σ below ref.
"2"	32.35	34	1.65	< one σ from ref.
"3"	32.55	31	1.55	< one σ from ref.

The result for digit "0" corresponds to one chance in 22.7.

The result for digit "1" corresponds to one chance in 24.4.
Both of these are probably significant.

Neither of the results for digit "2" or digit "3" are significant.

Base 4, soup, Patriarchs comparison, 3 column.

Finally, for base 4 calculations, a test was made using the four groups from the atmospheric noise source combined with the four groups from the Calculator Soup source assembled into a test of eight groups. In the following table (two sheets of illustration) the numbers in each group are paired; in each of the first three groups the number on the left hand side of the pair is from the atmospheric noise source and that on the right hand side is from the Calculator Soup program. For the fourth group the 'atmos' numbers are from the original '29 to 840' group and the 'soup' numbers are from the original 'C soup' group in the previous test. There were 32 separate pairs of equations in the line of best fit calculation and in the standard deviation calculation the total of squared differences was divided by 32 instead of 16.

The purpose of that was to test whether the figures for line of best fit and standard deviation for the foregoing calculations could be validly extrapolated to larger samples of groups of random numbers.

These next two sheets show the numbers that were used for the test of all five columns from the Excel files. The mid-point of the list of differences matched the (sigma x 0.6745) figure so no adjustment of standard deviation was required.

Digit	Group 1	Group 2	Group 3	Group 4
"0"	46 58	55 56	63 69	58 63
"1"	54 55	58 57	61 48	50 52
"2"	66 47	62 54	45 58	51 50
"3"	49 55	40 48	46 40	56 50

For these groups of numbers

The equation of the line of best fit is

$$Y = 58.5125 - 3.175X$$

The Standard Deviation is 5.94

Base 4 eight groups
random numbers, 5 columns

Digit	Ref.	Patriarch	Diff.	Significance
"0"	58.5125	82	23.4875	3.95 σ above ref.
"1"	55.3375	45	10.3375	1.74 σ below ref.
"2"	52.1625	44	8.1625	1.37 σ below ref.
"3"	48.9875	44	4.9875	< one σ from ref.

The result for digit "0" is almost certainly due to the non-random leading zeros in the 256s columns of the spread sheets.

The results for digits "1" and "2" are affected by the large negative slope on the line of best fit and are probably not significant.

The result for digit "3" is not significant.

Base 4 eight groups
Patriarch's comparison, 5 column.

This test of all five columns of the Excel files indicates as before the overwhelming effect of the leading zero function. The four column data (ignoring 256s columns) was expected to show a mix of the results for the five column and the three column tests so has not yet been tested.

The following two sheets show the figures that were used for the test of three columns (16s, 4s and units) of the same eight groups as previously.

Digit	Group 1	Group 2	Group 3	Group 4
"0"	29 33	35 32	36 40	30 34
"1"	36 29	34 31	38 25	31 28
"2"	34 31	34 34	22 35	31 27
"3"	30 36	26 32	33 29	37 40

For these groups of numbers

The equation of the line of best fit is

$$Y = 32.6625 - 0.275X$$

The unadjusted standard deviation is   4.01

The standard deviation is   4.24

Base 4 eight groups
random numbers, 3 columns

In the following "Patriarchs" comparison the use of the adjusted standard deviation means that the probability figures reported are slightly lower (less significant) than would be the case if the unadjusted figure was used. That is done so that the combined result of all the tests can be expressed as a 'not less than' figure. The most likely average result of many similar tests with different sets of random numbers would be expected to be much more significant.

Digit	Ref.	Patriarch	Diff.	Significance
"0"	32.6625	39	6.3375	1.49σ above ref.
"1"	32.3875	25	7.3875	1.74σ below ref.
"2"	32.1125	34	1.8875	< oneσ from ref.
"3"	31.8375	31	0.8375	< oneσ from ref.

The result for digit "0" corresponds to one chance in 14.7 and is of doubtful significance on its own.

The result for digit "1" corresponds to one chanced in 24.4 and is possibly significant.

The results for digits "2" and "3" are not significant.

Base 4 eight groups

patriartchs comparison 3 columns,

RESULTS OF THE BASE 4 CALCULATIONS

For the three column trials the results for digit zero are respectively; one chance in 17, one chance in 22.7 and one chance in 14.7; results for digit 1 are respectively; one chance in 65, one chance in 24.4 and another one with one chance in 24.4. The figures for digits 2 and 3 are consistently closer than one standard deviation to the reference and are not likely to be significant. The legally defendable results are one in 14.7 above the reference for digit zero and one in 24.4 below the reference for digit 1. We can expect that the trial of a large number of groups would yield results more significant than that. These figures indicate that generally results for line of best fit and standard deviation calculations on larger samples of similar groups will tend towards the average of all the smaller groups.

The one in 24.4 figure is in the, "probably significant" class. Because we will only ever have one set of patriarch's numbers to test we must look for tests with other base numbers to either confirm or deny this result.

BASE 5 CALCULATION

After the calculations detailed in the previous section for the base 4 investigation were completed an exactly similar procedure was commenced for testing the Patriarchs numbers translated into base 5. In the Excel program the column values are 625, 125, 25, 5 and 1. The leading zero factor was extreme; in the 625s column in all cases there were about 30 to 35 digit zeros the rest digit 1s and absolutely no 2s, 3s, or 4s.

I collected six groups of 43 numbers from the Random.org program and six groups from the Calculator Soup program. I used four groups for a test of numbers from the Random.org source and four groups from the Calculator Soup source for another test then used the remaining two groups from each source to make a test of a combined group.

The following three illustrations show numbers from the first four spread sheet calculations using numbers supplied by the Random.org (atmospheric noise) source. The first which shows numbers from all five columns was so obviously affected by the "0" and "1" digits in the 625s columns that work on it was stopped at that point.

Digit	Group 1	Group 2	Group 3	Group 4
"0"	63	72	70	73
"1"	64	48	38	51
"2"	26	35	38	25
"3"	39	27	30	36
"4"	23	33	39	30

In this test of all five columns the numbers were so strongly affected by the leading digit (0 or 1) that no further calculations were done on these groups.

Base 5 atmos. random numbers, 5 column

The second illustration which shows numbers collected from four columns (ignoring the 625s columns) is less severely affected and has some results which back up the results from the three column trial.

Digit	Group 1	Group 2	Group 3	Group 4
"0"	36	38	35	40
"1"	48	39	30	41
"2"	26	35	38	25
"3"	39	27	30	36
"4"	23	33	39	30

In these groups of numbers
The equation of the line of best fit is

$$Y = 38.2 - 1.9X$$

The unadjusted standard deviation is 5.58

The adjusted standard deviation is   5.26

Base 5 atmos. random numbers, 4 column

The results in the following sheet were calculated using the un-adjusted standard deviation.

Digit	Ref.	Patriarch	Diff.	Significance
"0"	38.2	66	27.8	4.98 σ above ref.
"1"	36.3	41	4.7	< one σ from ref.
"2"	34.4	27	7.4	1.33σ below ref.
"3"	32.5	21	11.5	2.06 σ below ref.
"4"	30.6	17	13.6	2.44 σ below ref.

The very high result for digit "0" is almost certainly an artefact of the significant excess of multiples of five in the plain language text of the Patriarch's ages.

The result for digit "1" is not significant.

The result for digit "2" (one chance in 10.7) is probably not significant.

The results for digit "3" (one chance in 49) and digit "4" (one in 134) are both in accordance with the three column test shown in the following two sheets.

Base 5 atmos.
Patriarch's comparison, 4 column

The test of three columns (25s, 5s and units) described in the next three illustrations used numbers from the same Excel files as the four column test above. These groups of numbers form a probability graph which is noticeably different from the true Gaussian distribution. The nominal half way point (0.6745 x sigma) is 3.0989; there are 12 numbers closer to the mean than that figure and only 8 further away. When the series is altered to make the distribution of numbers 10 either side of the line the standard deviation becomes 2.97.

That degree of adjustment is enough to cast doubt on the randomness of the groups of numbers originally supplied by the website however the same numbers in the four column trial above required less adjustment so the adjustment required for this test may be simply the exercise of a random probability related to the large number of individual tests in this series which is itself another Gaussian distribution.

Digit	Group 1	Group 2	Group 3	Group 4
"0"	26	26	24	27
"1"	35	27	22	31
"2"	21	27	26	20
"3"	33	23	25	27
"4"	14	26	32	24

For these groups of numbers
The equation of the line of best fit is

$$Y = 26.85 - 0.525X$$

The un-adjusted standard deviation is   4.59
The adjusted standard deviation is   2.97
Base 5 atmos. random numbers, 3 column

The comparison with Patriarchs stage of the calculation is in two forms; the first sheet deals with the un-adjusted figure for standard deviation and the second sheet is for the adjusted figure. Despite the doubt about the randomness of the original groups I am confident that the final figure for digit "4" is at least as significant as one chance in 102 and the figure for digit "3" is probably also significant.

Digit	Ref.	Pariarch	Diff.	Significance
"0"	26.85	47	20.15	4.39 σ above ref.
"1"	26.325	25	1.325	< one σ from ref.
"2"	25.8	26	0.2	< one σ from ref.
"3"	25.275	17	8.275	1.80 σ below ref.
"4"	24.75	14	10.75	2.34 σ below ref.

The very high result for digit "0" is almost certainly an artefact of the very large proportion of numbers in the plain language text which are divisible by 5.

The results for digits "1" and "2" are not significant.

The result for digit "3" corresponds to one chance in 27 and is possibly significant.

The result for digit "4" corresponds to one chance in 102 and is definitely significant.

Base 5 atmos.

Patriarchs comparison, unadjusted 3 column.

Digit	Ref.	Pariarch	Diff.	Significance
"0"	26.85	47	20.15	6.78 σ above ref.
"1"	26.325	25	1.325	< one σ from ref.
"2"	25.8	26	0.2	< one σ from ref.
"3"	25.275	17	8.275	2.79 σ below ref.
"4"	24.75	14	10.75	3.62 σ below ref.

The very high result for digit "0" is almost certainly an artefact of the very large proportion of numbers in the plain language text which are divisible by 5.

The results for digits "1" and "2" are not significant.

The result for digit "3" corresponds to one chance in 370 and is probably significant.

The result for digit "4" corresponds to one chance in approximately 3,000 and is definitely significant.

Base 5 atmos.

Patriarchs comparison, adjusted 3 column.

These next tests are of groups of numbers sourced from the Calculator Soup website (pseudo-random groups from a digital program) translated into base 5. In common with the trial of numbers from the atmospheric noise source the test of all five columns was severely affected by the non-random zeros in the 625s columns. The following table records those numbers. No calculations were done on them.

Digit	Group 1	Group 2	Group 3	Group 4
"0"	69	61	68	67
"1"	47	53	29	51
"2"	28	30	44	32
"3"	39	38	34	35
"4"	32	33	40	30

These figures show very strongly the effect of the non-random zeros in the 625s columns. No further calculations were done on these groups.

Base 5 soup,

random numbers, 5 columns.

The next two sheets show the calculation for four columns (ignoring 625s) of the same groups of random numbers. In this calculation the adjusted standard deviation is used to ensure that the final result will be at least as sure as the stated figures. This result is generally in accordance with the following trial of three columns of the same groups of random numbers.

Digit	Group 1	Group 2	Group 3	Group 4
"0"	42	30	31	37
"1"	31	41	23	38
"2"	28	30	44	32
"3"	39	38	34	35
"4"	32	33	40	30

For these numbers
The equation of the line of best fit is

$$Y = 34.25 + 0.075X$$

The un-adjusted standard deviation is 5.22
The adjusted standard deviation is   6.47

Base 5 soup
random numbers, 4 columns

This calculation uses the adjusted standard deviation.

Digit	Ref.	Patriarch	Diff.	Significance
"0"	34.25	66	31.75	4.9 **s** above ref.
"1"	34.325	41	6.675	< one σ from ref.
"2"	34.4	27	7.4	1.14 σ below ref.
"3"	34.475	21	13.375	2.08 σ below ref.
"4"	34.55	17	17.55	2.71 σ below ref.

The very high result for digit "0" is an artefact of The large proportion of numbers divisible by 5 in the plain language text.

The results for digits "1" and "2" are not significant.

The result for digit "3" corresponds to one chance in 51 and is probably significant.

The result for digit "4" corresponds to one chance in 287 and is definitely significant.

Base 5 soup
Patriarch's comparison, 4 column.

The next two sheets show calculations of a test of three columns (ignoring 625s and 125s columns). In this calculation the mid-point of a Gaussian distribution matches the middle of the differences list so no adjustment is required.

Digit	Group 1	Group 2	Group 3	Group 4
"0"	27	17	22	31
"1"	17	29	17	20
"2"	23	26	34	28
"3"	35	30	26	26
"4"	27	27	30	24

For these groups of numbers
The equation of the line of best fit is

$$Y = 23 + 1.4X$$

The standard deviation is 4.78

The mid-point of the differences list is at the
($\sigma \times 0.6745$) point.

Base 5 soup

random numbers, 3 columns.

Digit	Ref.	Patriarch	Diff,	Significance
"0"	23	47	24	5.02 σ above ref.
"1"	24.4	25	0.6	< one σ from ref.
"2"	25.8	26	0.2	< one σ from ref.
"3"	27.2	17	10.2	2.13 σ below ref.
"4"	28.6	14	14.6	3.04 σ below ref.

The very high result for digit "0" is an artefact of the large proportion of numbers divisible by 5 in the plain language text.

The results for digits "1" and "2" are not significant.

The result for digit "3" corresponds to one chance in 58 and is probably significant.

The result for digit "4" corresponds to one chance in 880 and is definitely significant.

Base 5 soup
Patriarchs comparison, 3 columns.

The above results have a particularly high level of certainty; there is good agreement between the four column and the three column calculations, the three column matches accurately with the theoretical Gaussian distribution and for the four column the adjustment required is minor.

In the following calculations two of the groups of numbers (A5 and A6) are from the Random.org website generated from atmospheric noise and the other two groups (S5 and S6) are from the Calculator Soup website generated by a digital program.

Digit	Group A 5	Group A 6	Group S 5	Group S 6
"0"	71	65	60	63
"1"	52	53	61	49
"2"	36	36	33	27
"3"	26	36	38	41
"4"	30	25	23	35

The 'leading zero' effect is very prominent in these figures and may be affecting the digit "1" figures as well. That is enough to mask any other relationships that may exist related to other digits.

No further calculations were done on these figures.

Base 5 combo,
random numbers, 5 columns.

Test of four columns (ignoring 625s column)

Digit	Group A 5	Group A 6	Group S 5	Group S 6
"0"	39	34	27	31
"1"	41	41	51	38
"2"	36	36	33	27
"3"	26	36	38	41
"4"	30	25	23	35

For these numbers
The equation of the line of best fit is

$$Y = 37.7 - 1.65X$$

The un-adjusted standard deviation is 6.26

The adjusted standard deviation is 7.34

Base 5 combo
random numbers, 4 columns,

This calculation uses the adjusted standard deviation.

Digit	Ref.	Patriarch	Diff.	Significance
"0"	37.7	66	28.3	3.86 σ above ref.
"1"	36.05	41	4.95	< one σ from ref.
"2"	34.4	27	7.4	1.01 σ below ref.
"3"	32.75	21	11.75	1.60 σ below ref.
"4"	31.1	17	14.1	1.92 σ below ref.

The very high result for digit "0" is an artefact of the large proportion of the plain language numbers that are divisible by 5.

The results for digits "1" and "2" are not significant.

The result for digit "3" may not be significant.

The result for digit "4" corresponds to one chance in 57 and is probably significant.

Base 5 combo,
Patriarch's comparison, 4 columns

The results of this test of four columns are basically in accordance with the following test of three columns however in contrast to the trial using numbers from the Calculator Soup website reported above this test adds little to the certainty of the three columns trial shown below.

Test of three columns (25s, 5, and units) of random numbers from the same groups as above.

Digit	Group A 5	Group A 6	Group S 5	Group S 6
"0"	30	22	17	18
"1"	28	31	35	25
"2"	27	29	26	22
"3"	20	27	34	35
"4"	24	20	17	29

For these groups of numbers
The equation of the line of best fit is

$$Y = 25.65 + 0.075X$$

The un-adjusted standard deviation is 5.59
The adjusted standard deviation is   6.04

Base 5 combo
random numbers, 3 columns.

This calculation uses the un-adjusted standard deviation.

Digit	Ref.	Patriarch	Diff.	Significance
"0"	25.65	47	21.35	3.82 σ above ref.
"1"	25.725	25	0.725	< one σ from ref.
"2"	25.8	26	0.2	< one σ from ref.
"3"	25.875	17	8.875	1.59 σ below ref.
"4"	25.95	14	11.95	2.14 σ below ref.

The very high result for digit "0" is an artefact of of the large proportion of the plain language numbers divisible by 5.

The results for digits "1" and "2" are not significant.

The result for digit "3" corresponds to one chance in 17 and is probably not significant on its own.

The result for digit "4" corresponds to one chance in 59 and is probably significant.

Base 5 combo
Patriarchs comparison un-adjusted, 3 columns.

This calculation uses the adjusted
standard deviation.

Digit	Ref.	Patriarch	Diff.		Significance
"0"	25.65	47	21.35	3.53	above ref.
"1"	25.725	25	0.725	< one	from ref.
"2"	25.8	26	0.2	< one	from ref.
"3"	25.875	17	8.875	1.47	below ref.
"4"	25.95	14	11.95	1.98	below ref.

The very high result for digit "0" is an artefact of
the very large proportion of the numbers in the
plain language text that are divisible by 5.

The results for digits "1" and "2" are not significant.

The result for digit "3" corresponds to one chance in
14 which is probably not significant by itself.

The result for digit "4" corresponds to one chance
in 41 which is probably significant.

Base 5 combo
Patriarchs comparison, adjusted, 3 columns.

ROUND UP

In the base 5 form the three column tests show
consistently very high results for digit 0 and figures below
reference for digits 3 and 4. The high results for digit 0 are all
artefacts of the highly significant association with the number
5 in the original list of the Patriarchs ages.

For digit 3 the results are respectively; one chance in
370, one chance in 58 and one chance in 14. The one chance
in 14 is the legally defendable figure but the true result of
testing a very big number of groups is almost certainly much
more certain than that.

For digit 4 the results are respectively; one chance in 3,000, one chance in 880 and one chance in 41. The last is the legally defendable figure but as for digit 3 the true result of testing a very large number of groups is almost certainly much more significant than that.

The possibility was raised of an 'end effect' modifying the result for digit 4. Of the 12 reference groups tested the figure for digit 4 was greater than the related digit 3 in four out of the 12 cases. In the three column tests the slope of the line of best fit was downward in one case and upward in the other two. Within the limits of experimental error, it is not possible to definitely establish that an end effect either does or does not occur but we can say that the magnitude of the effect if it exists would be small.

ASSOCIATIONS BETWEEN NUMBERS

I think it is significant to look at the Bible numeric meanings of the numbers involved.

The number 4 is associated with "The natural creation".

The number 1 is associated with "The presence of God" among other things".

The number 5 is associated with "The grace of God".

In relation to the chemical elements there are clear groupings of Bible code numbers. There is also an indirect suggestion that the digit "0" which does not have an association in the traditional numerics list may be associated with the lake of eternal fire (or the 'second death') described in Revelation chapter 19 and 20. The book "You were designed

– the code is in your chemicals" ISBN 9781940269238 deals with the pairing and grouping of numbers in section 8.6 on its page 129. There is also information on the significance of zero in sections 3.3 and 3.4 on page 47 of that book.

The association of the number 4 with the number 6 suggested by the early results is quite clearly indicated in relation to the chemical elements and the significance of zero as the final end of the natural creation (number 4) is clearly described in Revelation chapter 20.

From the standpoint of the final judgement it is reasonable to expect that the natural creation (number 4) could have a negative association with the presence of God (number 1) and a positive association with the lake of fire (number 0) exactly as shown by these calculations. It is also reasonable to expect a negative association between the natural creation and the grace of God as shown by the base 5 calculation.

Q.E.D.

The original purpose of this exercise was to try to find a less easily fabricated relationship in the Patriarchs numbers. The probability of finding both this base 4 and this base 5 result in the same set of Patriarchs ages is 1/24.4 x 1/41 = 1/1,001 of this being achieved by random chance.

This is still a work in progress; eventually I will try the same set of calculations using some of the other base numbers – if the Lord does not return beforehand and reveal the final truth thereby removing the need for more search.

UPDATE TO END OF JUNE 2020

BASE 6, BASE 7 AND BASE 9

Statisticians generally regard any result that indicates a chance of larger (smaller number) than one in 20 as being of doubtful significance; for results in the range one in 20 to one in 100 as 'probably significant' and for results more significant than one in 100 as 'definitely significant'.

To the end of June 2020 comparisons have been made for the Patriarchs numbers compared to random numbers expressed in base 4, base 5, base 6, base 7 and base 9. In each case two groups of calculations have been done; one group of random numbers has been supplied from the Random.org website and one group of random numbers from the Calculator soup integer generator website. This list shows all those cases where a particular digit expressed in a particular base number recorded a result more significant than one chance in 20. (Note that the result could be that the digit occurred significantly more often than the random reference, described as 'above reference' or the digit could have occurred significantly less often than random, described as 'below reference'.)

Expressed in base 4 the "0" digit was highly significantly above reference in the test of all five columns but the cause was due to the effect of the non-random leading zero.

For random numbers supplied by the 'Calculator soup' program, in the test of the three least significant columns where the leading zero factor is removed digit "0" was above the reference and had a chance of one in 22.7; digit "1" was below the reference with chance of one in 24.4

For the corresponding test with random numbers supplied by the Random.org website, in the test of three least significant columns the probability for digit "0" was one chance in 17 above the reference and the figure for digit "1" was one chance in 65 below the reference.

Expressed in base 5 the "0" digit was significantly above reference for all tests due to an artefact of the number 5 which has a significance in the plain language text.

In reference to random numbers supplied by the 'Calculator soup' program in the test of the three least significant columns; digit "3" was below reference with a probability of one chance in 58 and digit "4" was below reference with probability of one chance in 880.

With random numbers supplied by the Random.org website a similar test of the three least significant columns indicated that digit "3" was below reference with probability of one chance in 370 and digit "4" was also below reference with probability smaller than one chance in 3,000. This result however is in context of groups of reference numbers which resulted in a significant discrepancy from the true Gaussian distribution.

When expressed in base 6 all the Patriarch's numbers smaller than 216 will be affected by the leading zero factor so ˋst of all four columns was not attempted. In a test of three ˋ using random numbers supplied by the Random.org ˋ "5" was above reference with probability of one chance in 45; the figure for the corresponding test with numbers supplied by the Calculator soup website was one chance in 10.7.

When expressed in base 7 all the Patriarch's numbers smaller than 343 are affected by the leading zero factor. When the three least significant digits were compared with random numbers supplied by the 'Calculator soup' program digit "1" gave a result which was above reference with a chance of one in 20.7; digit "2" gave a result which was above reference with probability of approximately one chance in 2,500; digit 5 was below reference with probability of one chance in 28 and digit "6" was also below reference with probability of one chance in 570.

The set of numbers supplied by the Random.org website for a test corresponding to the above formed a distinctly non-Gaussian probability distribution. When it was adjusted to be correct at the half way mark the following probability figures were recorded.

Digit "2" was above reference with probability of one chance in 39 and digit "6" was below reference with probability of one chance in 32. Digit "1" was above reference but not significantly and digit "5" had probability of one chance in 12.7 below reference.

If the above adjustment is not applied the probability figures become:-

- For digit "2" one chance in 250
- For digit "5" one chance in 34
- For digit "6" one chance in 190.

When the numbers are expressed in base 9 all below 729 are subject to the leading zero factor. For a test of three columns comparing with random numbers supplied by the Random.org website digit "2" showed a probability of one chance in 35; digit "4" showed probability of one chance in 308 below reference and digit "6" showed probability of one chance in 28 also below reference.

For a similar test of three columns using numbers supplied by the Calculator soup website digit "2" probability was one chance in 21; digit "4" one chance in 73 and digit "6" one chance in 17.4.

In each of these results the legally defendable figure is the smallest (least significant) number for each test however it is also legally defendable that the probability of all these results coming from one set of Bible references is found by multiplying all those results of individual tests together and that is an extremely small possibility.

God however is not interested in legal proof of anything but He is interested in providing enough evidence for a willingly open minded person to form a conclusion based on probabilities.

In relation to Bible numeric concepts the number 4 which is associated with, 'natural creation' is clearly negatively associated with number 5 and number 9 and possibly positively associated with number zero. The preliminary test suggested that the number 9 is also negatively associated with number 16 which is 4 squared.

In the traditional Bible coding number 0 is not included but it may possibly be associated with the lake of fire described in Revelation chapter 20. If the, 'finality' associated with number 9 can be applied to the finality of the judgment of Revelation chapter 20 then all these associations with the number 4 are in accordance with the Bible's coding.

For the number 5 which in the Bible is associated with, 'God's grace'; in these tests all the results other than for the number 4 are in the, 'probably significant class'. It is positively associated with number 6 and negatively associated with number 3 and number 7. At first glance this seems surprising; numbers 3 and 7 are both numbers associated with God. My suggestion is that the grace of God is all to do with giving mankind a second chance or diluting the effect of God's justice; number 7 at least is associated with God's justice in its full severity.

For the number 6 it is positively associated with the number 5 as explained above and negatively associated with the numbers 7 and 9. All these are in accordance with the concepts associated with the Bible code.

For the number 7 there is a possible positive association with number 1, a very definite positive association with number 2 and negative associations with numbers 5 and 6. The Bible numeric concept for number 2 includes, 'sanctification' and for number 7 it is, among other things, the cleaning and disinfecting power of the Holy Spirit. In that sense all these associations are in accordance with the Bible code.

For the number 9 these tests showed a probably significant positive association with the number 2, a very clear negative association with number 4 and a probable negative association with number 6. All these are in accordance with Bible coding.

* * * * * *
.. ..

The importance of this is not just that by mathematical procedures some figures can be produced that seem to indicate a list that was designed for that purpose but also that when those figures are identified they fit in with and verify a list of concepts that were derived by Biblical scholars about 120 years ago.

At that time the probability theory that this work is based on was not used for testing of scientific discoveries; it only existed in a rudimentary form in gambling dens and at race tracks – places which Bible scholars did not respect.

Note also that this list of numbers from the dawn of recorded history has reference through the numbers 4 and 9 to the end of the natural Universe.

THE END

?

Well not really; actually it's more like

THE BEGINNING

There is a lot more of the story still to be discovered!

If you seek to check these calculations, I encourage you to obtain another set of random numbers for each calculation. If you do that the results you get will not exactly match my figures but in most cases they should follow the same pattern and definitely significant results in my calculations should be matched with results in the same class for yours.

Chapter 12: The Big Picture

The subject of Bible numerics is at the centre of the spiritual war between God and Satan. For practically any other subject that may be the focus of a scientific investigation, such as growth rates of crops and plants, tempering of metals or any of the many thousands of physical and chemical processes that are at the centre of modern technology, the collection of clearly non-random number gems listed here would be the basis of whole industries to improve the lives of the general population of the World. The fight is not just in the supernatural dimension however; egos and prejudices get in the road and for this subject everybody has an ego and many people have prejudices. This exercise bears directly on the existence or otherwise of the supernatural dimension and that is a subject that everybody who has ever lived has or had a life or death interest in.

The search that I have conducted over the last 42 years has identified a number of provably non-random facts in three parts of the overall subject of Bible numerics. The three parts of the subject are very small but they are selected almost at random so there is an implication that a similar search in other parts of the scriptures would uncover more facts of the same types. I am someone who always wanted to believe in a supernatural God so for me these three examples are quite sufficient for me to proclaim them as evidence that the Bible is not a natural book that the supernatural God that it writes about is real and that Jesus Christ did physically live on our Earth, he died a real death and was raised from being dead to real physical life. By demonstrating that, Jesus showed that it is also possible for God to raise us from the dead after our natural life is finished.

I am very aware that not everybody shares my opinion. When I was young I had a cousin who was older than me who I greatly admired. He was an expert on industrial chemistry and devoted his life to making and selling agricultural chemicals, mainly fertilizers and weedicides. He had been generally not interested in our God. At the end of his life he was in hospital suffering from a stomach cancer. I visited him to try to interest him in the chemical facts of Bible numerics. He listened politely but at the end of it his summation was, "They had some very clever fellows in those days, didn't they!" He died a few days later.

The three subjects that I have investigated are like three threads of a vast and incredibly intricate tapestry of number related patterns which through the written word of God in the Bible connects the natural world with the supernatural. The writing of the Bible is inspired and the author of that inspiration is someone who is many hundreds or thousands of times more intellectually powerful than the smartest human being who ever lived. There is a lot more about it yet to be discovered, probably several lifetimes worth of investigation.

The tapestry itself is mainly hidden but there are a few places where bits of it can be seen and these bits can be entry points for investigation. For the investigators however we must all insist that the probability calculation is the key and until you have a genuinely non-random pattern you have nothing of any value.

Appendix 1 contains an extract from the Greek text of the Third Epistle of John from both the Interlinear New Testament and the British And Foreign Bible Society's Ancient Greek New Testament. It also contains the words as written in the Strong's Concordance and the table of numeric values of the Greek characters copied from the book, "Number In Scripture" by E. W. Bullinger. That should give you enough information to reconstruct the calculations I did at first. If you want to check the more basic principles on which the calculations are based all those books are recommended as sources of information.

Appendix 2 contains contact information about the book, "You Were Designed – The Code Is In Your Chemicals". There are several reliable sources of information about the properties of individual elements and I recommend that you make an assessment of that book based on your own independent research.

Appendix 3 details the procedure I used to produce the random number reference figures that I used to compare with the 'Ages of the Patriarchs' figures.

Appendix 4 is a list of all the number patterns found so far which give results clearly more significant than one chance in 100 of being a random result. It has the effect of being a summary of the results so far of my 42 years of search.

If you are someone who feels the urge to strike out on your own, picking on a part that has not yet been explored to do calculations similar to what has been described in this book the field is wide open, you are welcome to explore; however, if you do please be rigorous in your research. You have nothing proven until you have done the probability calculation. There are plenty of eye-catching 'facts' available to distract attention and if all you do is display those without any real proof you are playing Satan's game and given time you will discredit the whole concept of Bible numerics. I trust that you will find many things where real proof is available and can be demonstrated.

The 43 numbers detailing the patriarchs, their ages and their children's ages are a special group of numbers that can be treated on their own and have yielded very significant results. Genesis chapter 5 and chapter 11 are not the only places where groups of numbers such as that are present. There is a similar group of numbers in chapter 2 of the book of Ezra in which the number one hundred and twenty-eight is listed twice which by itself is a notably unexpected event. 128 = 2^7 and the plain language story is about a party of Israelites returning to Jerusalem to rebuild the Temple. The factors "2" and "7" are positively matched to the spiritual aspects of that work.

There also appears to be a non-random sequence of facts surrounding the time period of forty years related to the leaders and kings of the Old Testament tribes.

There is an overriding fact that hangs over all this and actually applies equally to all subjects of this type. It is only of interest to a very small proportion of people somewhere between one in a thousand and one in ten thousand. On the world scale those numbers translate into somewhere between 750 thousand and seven and a half million people of the present World population. The difficulty is that all are strangers, I don't know who they are and in most cases they don't know who each other are. The problem is to find those people without wasting time and making a nuisance to the other 99.9% of people who are not interested.

With this particular subject there is an added complication that everybody has a prejudice one way or the other about God. Some people, like me, want to have a God even when they can't find Him, others actively (and sometimes belligerently) want to have no God and can be quite offended by being told about Him. Between those two extremes there are a range of attitudes and we all have an attitude which we want to hang on to. Almost everybody is emotionally involved in one way or another; there are no unbiased observers.

There are two questions which you as an individual need to ask and you as an individual need to answer for yourself. Do you want to believe in a supernatural God? Do you want the eternal life that He seeks to offer you?

If you have answered, "No" to either of these questions I have very little to offer you; I have no particular wish to muck up your life, enjoy it as much as you can, it's the only one you will have!

If you have answered, "Yes" to these questions be wholehearted about it; the answer may be your key to eternal life. These are questions you must answer for yourself, don't take my suggestion without checking. Please do not ask other peoples' opinions, if you do you will get a political consensus which will almost certainly include the opinions of some people who would answer, "No". Your chance of eternal life depends on your personal relationship with God not on a political group opinion. Please do not allow yourself to be tricked by a religious god; there are over 3,000 official gods in the World as well as money, football and personal achievement and all except one are dead imitations. It is tremendously important that you do not accept anything I have written without working through the calculations and checking them for yourself.

In the background of this search for significant number patterns there has also been a second search going on. I spent about the first 40 to 50 years of my life trying to pretend to myself that I was a nice normal human being but it never really worked. I continually found that ideas that I thought were most significant or most valuable were not particularly of interest to other people around me and conversely the big issues for the vast majority of people were often pretty irrelevant to me. Even after I found the God who answers by fire and got involved with His people I am still a bit of a weirdo; but I cling to the conviction that I am not the only one. I haven't found the others yet. If after reading this book you know of someone who thinks in numbers will you please pass this on to them.

Appendix 1

The Interlinear Bible has the Greek text (for the New Testament) on one line and a word based translation immediately below it. I did not attempt a numeric test of the title words. In the Greek the title is; first word (Epsilon, Pi, Iota, Sigma, Tau, Omicron, Lambda, Eta), second word (Iota, Omega, Alpha, Nu, Nu, Omicron, Upsilon), third word (Tau, Rho, Iota, Tau, Eta). The interlinear translation is:-

EPISTLE _ OF _ JOHN _ THIRD

The first sentence is:-

Ο πρεσβυτερος Γαιψ τψ αγαπητψ ον εγω
The   elder   to Gaius the   beloved whom I

αγαπω εν αληθεια.
  love   in   truth.

The third sentence is:-

εχαρην.γαρ   λιαν   ερχομενων αδελφων
For I rejoiced exceedingly coming [the] brethren

και μαρτυρουντων σου τη αληθεια, καθως
and bearing witness   of   thy   truth, Even as

συ εν αληθεια περιπατεις.
thou in   truth   walkest.

Note: in one manuscript identified as, "T[Tr]" (gamma, alpha, rho) is missing from the first word of the third sentence.

These were the two sentences that were most outstanding for me. If you wish to check my calculations for the whole book it is, "Interlinear Greek – English New Testament" by George Ricker Berry, published by Baker Book House, Grand Rapids, Michigan, USA. The ISBN is 0-8010-0700-3.

In the British and Foreign Bible Society's Greek New Testament sentence 1 reads:-

First word (Omicron); second word, all uppercase (Pi, Rho, Epsilon, Sigma, Upsilon, Tau, Epsilon, Rho, Omicron, Sigma); third word (Gamma, alpha, iota, omega); fourth word (tau, omega); fifth word (alpha, gamma, alpha, pi, eta, tau, omega); sixth word (omicron, nu); seventh word (epsilon, gamma, omega); eighth word (alpha, gamma, alpha, pi, omega) ninth word (epsilon, nu); tenth word (alpha, lambda, eta, theta, epsilon, iota, alpha).

Sentence 3 reads:-

First word (epsilon, chi, alpha, rho, eta, nu); second word (gamma, alpha, rho); third word (lambda, iota, alpha, nu); fourth word (epsilon, rho, chi, omicron, mu, epsilon, omega, nu); fifth word (alpha, delta, epsilon, lambda, phi, omega, nu); sixth word (kappa, alpha, iota); seventh word (mu, alpha, rho, tau, upsilon, rho, omicron, upsilon, nu, tau, omega, nu); eighth word (sigma, omicron, nu); ninth word (tau, eta); tenth word (alpha, lambda, eta, theta, epsilon, iota, alpha); eleventh word (kappa, alpha, theta, omega, stigma); twelfth word (sigma, upsilon); thirteenth word (epsilon, nu); fourteenth word (alpha, lambda, eta, theta, epsilon, iota, alpha); fifteenth word (pi, epsilon, rho, iota, pi, alpha, tau, epsilon, iota, stigma).

The title of the book is all uppercase, "Eta, Kappa, Alpha, Iota, Nu, Eta, Delta, Iota, Alpha, Theta, Eta, Kappa, Eta" published by the British and Foreign Bible Society. ISBN is 0 564 02049 4.

Strong's Concordance does not list all the equivalent words; the ones that are listed are:-

For sentence 1

Elder = (pi, rho, epsilon, sigma, beta, upsilon, tau, epsilon, rho, omicron, stigma); same as Interlinear

well-beloved = (alpha, gamma, alpha, pi, eta, tau, omicron, stigma); different from both

Gaius = (Gamma, alpha, iota, omicron, stigma); different from both

Love = (alpha, gamma, alpha, pi, alpha, omega); different from both

Truth = (alpha, lambda, eta, theta, epsilon, iota, alpha); same as both.

For sentence 3

Rejoiced = (chi, alpha, iota, rho, omega); different from both

greatly = (lambda, iota, alpha, nu); same as both

brethren = (alpha, delta, epsilon, lambda, phi, omicron, stigma); different from both

came = (epsilon, rho, chi, omicron, mu, alpha, iota); different from both

testified = (mu, alpha, rho, tau, upsilon, rho, epsilon, omega); different from both

truth = (alpha, lambda, eta, theta, epsilon, iota, alpha); same as both

The number equivalents I used for the characters were:-

Alpha α = 1	Iota	ι = 10	Rho ρ = 100
Beta β = 2	Kappa κ	= 20	Sigma σ = 200
Gamma γ = 3	Lambda λ = 30	Tau τ = 300
Delta δ = 4	Mu	μ = 40	Upsilon υ = 400
Epsilon ε = 5	Nu	ν = 50	Phi ϕ = 500
Stigma s = 6	Xi	ξ = 60	Chi χ = 600
Zeta ζ = 7	Omicron o = 70	Psi ψ = 700
Eta η = 8	Pi	π = 80	Omega ω = 800
Theta θ = 9			

For 90 there was a character similar to the English upper case G called, "Koppa".

For 900 there was a character similar to the lower case Greek omega rotated anticlockwise 135° called, "Sampsi".

Appendix 2

"You Were Designed – The Code Is In Your Chemicals" is a book about codes and a mystery!

Two sets of numbers that should be from totally unrelated sources show a very high correlation. WHY?

If you live in Australia, you should be able to borrow a copy from your local public library. In other parts of the World the publisher is Deep River Books, P O Box 310, Sisters, Oregon 97759, USA. They have a website www.deepriverbooks.com. ISBN for the book is 9781940269238.

In addition to the major subject of that book which deals with the chemical elements there are references to some places where the World's gem stones are referred to in the Bible. Section 9.8 starting on page 145 has information about the High Priest's breast plate and refers to the obviously non-random, in the chemical sense, layout of the gem stones. The following section 9.9 deals with the list of stones in the symbolic New Jerusalem of the book of Revelation.

The pearl is the only gemstone which is made by a living organism; chemically it is calcium carbonate which is related to the numbers 2 (calcium), 4 (carbon) and 6 (oxygen). The word, 'pearl' is used twice in the Bible; There is the parable of the, 'pearl of great price' in which the Kingdom of God is described as a pearl; and the description of the gates of the New Jerusalem. In both these references the story is about 'separation and sanctification' which is the numeric significance of the number 2. There are some other references to groups of pearls but these two are the only places where a pearl is treated as a singular item.

To independently check the properties of the chemical elements it is probably best to consult good quality printed encyclopaedias searching for individual elements by name. Some information is available on websites but the internet has information that is basically uncontrolled so may be of doubtful reliability. Internet information is valuable when it corroborates other sources and/or leads to reliable data.

The major source of information about the scriptural significance of numbers has been from the book, "Number In Scripture" by E. W. Bullinger, originally published in 1894 and reprinted many times since then. My copy was printed in 1979 by Kregel Publications, Grand Rapids, Michigan 49501, U S A. ISBN is 0-8254-2204-3. There was some data collected directly from a King James Version Bible, mine is a Thompson Chain Reference Bible printed by the B B Kirkbride company. There have also been many conversations with associates in the Fellowship who have studied various aspects of the subject.

Instruction in statistical techniques was from the book, "Facts From Figures" by M J Moroney published by Penguin Books. My copy was from the third edition dated 1956 and printed in 1962. In modern times there are programmable calculators that can handle all those calculations.

Appendix 3

To produce the random number sets for a reference to compare with the patriarch's numbers I used the following procedure.

Step 1; from the relevant website collect a group of random numbers. 43 numbers with minimum value 28 and maximum value 841. These are supplied in normal base 10 form.

Step 2; use the spread sheet program to present those numbers in the base you are currently working in. The output of that program is presented in columns with an individual digit in each column for each number in the group. There are five columns for base 4 and base 5, four columns for bases 6 to 9 and three columns for bases 10 to 16.

Step 3; count and record the number of appearances of each digit in each column.

Step 4; from those figures total and record the sum of all appearances of each digit in all of the columns. Make a separate similar list of all the appearances of each digit in all columns except the most significant column and if appropriate make a third list in which the two most significant columns are ignored.

Step 5; store those results in a safe place then repeat steps 1 to 4 for other groups of random numbers as many times as required for your test. (In my case four times and later six times)

Step 6; collect all the stored results into a table similar to that shown at (Kindle 69%).

Step 7; calculate a line of best fit. The book, "Facts From Figures" shows three methods of calculating a 'least squares' line of best fit. The method I used was for each point on the table generate two equations. In the first ($Y = mx + c$) the number of appearances of a digit is the "Y" value, the digit number is the "X" value, the "c" will eventually be the Y axis intercept and the "m" will eventually be the slope of the line. The second equation is the first ($Y = mx + c$) with each term multiplied by the digit number (X value). Sum the individual terms of each of the equations to produce two final equations then use the simultaneous equations process to evaluate a final figure for each of the "c" and "m" terms. Once these values are available the line of best fit can be presented as an equation in terms of "Y" and "X".

Step 8; calculate a standard deviation of all the individual digit appearance numbers in the table. Use the calculated line of best fit as the reference, calculate an individual difference figure for each digit appearance and square each of those difference figures. Take an arithmetic average of all the squared difference figures then the standard deviation is the square root of that average.

Step 9; I used an extra procedure to check the degree of randomness of the groups of numbers originally collected from the website. For a true Gaussian 'normal' graph half of the individual data points should be closer to the reference than 0.6745 times the standard deviation. I multiplied the calculated figure by 0.6745 then looked back at the 'differences' list to count how many of the differences were smaller than that figure. In some cases I calculated an adjustment for the standard deviation and used the adjusted figure for the final probability calculation.

Step 10; present the patriarch's numbers in the base you are working on (steps 1 to 4) and count the total number of appearances of each digit and compare with the calculated line of best fit. Use the calculated standard deviation figure to derive a probability figure for each number of digit appearances. All figures that are closer than one standard deviation to the reference are insignificant, figures closer than 1.65 times the standard deviation are not significant by themselves but may be contributors to an overall result in association with other figures and all figures larger than 2.36 times the standard deviation are definitely significant on their own.

Appendix 4: Numerical gemstones discovered so far

The result of a set of calculations can be counted as a God's gem if the probability of the least certain result of all the separate sums has less chance than one in 100 of being a random result. The following is a list of those that my calculations have uncovered so far. In the future many more will be found by other investigators researching other parts of the scriptures.

(Kindle 15%)

Third Epistle of John, sum of the gematria of the first sentence total 6272. Factors 2 and 7; probability one chance in 224.

(Kindle 33%)

38 out of 94 chemical elements show a strong and clear match between the number of their electrons that can take part in chemical reactions and their properties related to the Bible numeric properties of that number. Sigma value of probability is 7.2; probability is approx. one in 20 million.

Chapter 7; (Kindle 34%)

15 out of the 21 elements essential for life are in the class of those strongly associated with Bible numeric numbers. Conversely of the 4 elements which have a negative association to the numeric code none are required for life and all can be toxic under certain circumstances.

Chapter 8; (Kindle 38%)

In the patriarch's numbers in Genesis chapter 5 and chapter 11; 28 of the 43 numbers are divisible by 5 and 8 are divisible by 100. Probability is approx. one chance in 30 million.

(Kindle 41% and Kindle 49%)

In the base 5 presentation, using numbers supplied by the Calculator Soup website digit 4 is below reference with more certainty than one chance in 880.

(Kindle 49%)

In the base 7 presentation digit 2 was above reference with probability of one chance in approx. 2,500 and digit 6 was below reference with probability of one chance in 570.

Of these seven examples all are in accordance with the relevant Bible numeric meanings of numbers.

I hope this will be a basis for further discussion and investigation.

Over to the next investigator.

OTHER BOOKS BY THE SAME AUTHOR.

"HOW RADIO SIGNALS WORK" Published by McGraw-Hill

Australian print date 14 – 4 – 1996, ISBN 0 07 470329 3
USA print date 22 – 2 – 1998, ISBN original (ten digit) 007-058058-9; recent (thirteen digit) 9780070580589.

A book that deals specifically with the radio signal itself with minimum consideration of the electronics inside the transmitter and receiver boxes.

"RADIO SIGNAL FINDING" Published by TAB Electronics, McGraw-Hill USA

Print date 2001, ISBN 0-07-137191-5.

This book was intended to be of value to people with limited technical understanding who are required to achieve a technical function in an isolated environment. Also of value to everyone who has a responsibility for or is interested in radio technology in less extreme circumstances.

"YOU WERE DESIGNED – THE CODE IS IN YOUR CHEMICALS"

Published in USA by Deep River Books, print date 2014, ISBN 9781940269238.

This is a book about codes and a mystery. Two sets of numbers that should be from totally unrelated sources show a very high correlation. Why?

This book injects some basic data into a highly emotionally charged subject.

ABOUT THE AUTHOR

The "I" mentioned frequently in this text is Jim Sinclair a resident of an outer southern suburb of Adelaide, South Australia for the last 40 years.

For most of my working life I have been involved in radio technology in one form or another. The day I first started work for the Australian PMGs Department the Supervising Technician told me, "In this game it pays to know as much as you can about everything except radio!" His point was that all the purely radio issues are worked out by engineers and their helpers and we are left with the practical problems of all other types that need to be solved to make the system work.

I soon found that I was continually dealing with numbers ._.for measurements ._. for calculating component values; and for a host of other purposes.

42 years ago someone told me about the numeric code built into the Bible. It is an incredibly intricate and complex code of numbers; this book, definitely 'everything except radio', deals with three aspects of it. There is a lot more to be found; if you wish to investigate – good hunting!

jimlsinclair@bigpond.com